THE ULTIM… A FOODI DUA… R FRYER COOKBOOK … RS

1000 Vibrant and Delicious Ninja 2-Basket Air Fryer Recipes for Your Ninja Foodi Dual Zone Air Fryer

KATHLEEN C. MARTINS

MAX CRISP
AIR FRY
ROAST
BAKE
REHEAT
DEHYDRATE
TEMP
1
TEMP
2

Table of Contents

Introduction

Your entire life, you have been fed with a deception that If you use the Ninja Dual Zone Air Fryer for fried meals,they turn out to be unhealthy. On the contrary, this device is endowed with so many options for tasty, crunchy, and healthful meals that it might be overwhelming.By moving hot air around the food, the Ninja Dual Zone Air Fryer cooks your meal while using very little oil and fat. The danger of acrylamide production as a result of deep frying, which also results in breast, oesophageal, cervical, and endometrial cancer, is reduced by this procedure.

Since the days have been so busy, cooking has not been an option. The Ninja Foodi Dual Zone Air Fryer answers your dilemma if you ever wished for tasty and healthy meals. Among the many types of air fryers, the Ninja Foodi Dual Zone Air Fryer is a recent addition. The most admired feature of this air fryer is its dual basket design, which enables the cooking of two separate dishes with dual settings that might be distinct or similar.Compared to an air fryer with just one basket, it is different. People who desire tasty, healthy dishes with a crackling surface but with less fat as a goal for this appliance. A great device to meet all of your culinary needs is the Ninja Foodi Dual Zone Air Fryer. With the Ninja Dual Zone Air Fryer, you can prepare delicious meals that are equal to those seen in eateries.

For just about any celebration or picnic, you can make a different cuisine. Food preparation modes on the Ninja Foodi Dual Zone Air Fryer include max crisp, air fry, roast, reheat, dehydrate, and bake. One appliance offers every useful feature. Meals can be baked or dried without the need for additional equipment. Using this device, you can roast beef, fish, fowl and vegetables. Using the bake mode, you can make a cake, muffin, cupcake, or pancake, reheating leftovers, dehydrating vegetables for crisps, and for frying frozen foods like nuggets and fries, select maximum crisp.

The benefits and attractions of this ground-breaking appliance will be covered in this cookbook for the Ninja Foodi Dual Zone Air Fryer. In addition, this cookbook discusses how to use the Ninja Foodi Dual Zone Air Fryer to its fullest capacity. I will show you a range of recipes that can be used on the dailies. It's not difficult to utilize the air fryer. You may confidently create delectable cuisine for your family and friends after you grasp how to use the Ninja Foodi Dual Zone Air Fryer.

1000 Delicious, Stress-Free Recipes for Air Frying, Max Crisping, Roasting, Baking, Reheating, and Dehydrating. Easy, delectable recipes for your favorite fried foods that are speedier, healthy, and crunchier.

Chapter 1
Basics of the Ninja Dual Zone Air Fryer

The Ninja Dual Zone Air Fryer Design

There is sufficient visual appeal for surface display.

Although I wouldn't necessarily describe this fryer as elegant, it does include some appealing design elements, including rounded edges, metal framing, and dark grey panels that appear understated and classic.

Given that meals will have to be stirred or swirled somewhat while cooking, the front handlebars are perfect because they are large and comfortable to hold. Additionally, they are the ideal shape and size required for taking cooked food out of the basket effortlessly. The fryer should fit under cabinets as long as it is not in use considering its height.

There were a couple occasions when I wasn't sure what to do, despite the controls being simple. A Start/Pause button allowed me to pause cooking on each side of the fryer, but I chose to halt the process when food on one side got ready earlier than I had anticipated. The Time function was employed as the remedy to alert the fryer that the cooking time was up. Although it wasn't evident right away, that was efficient.

It was easy to adjust the cooking duration, but I had to read the manual to understand the Smart Finish and Match settings.

I thought there should have been more instruction provided about how to utilize the crisper trays that go in the bottom of the baskets. They do, in my opinion, improve air circulation for air frying, but I was not certain about the sorts of recipes that would not need the bottom heat. I made use of the trays even when I fried a few cookies. For the bulk or most of my air fryer meals, I'll probably still use these regardless of the fact that they all have perforations and a not too smooth surface because of the handle.

Prior to the Initial Use

- Remove any ribbon, tags, and wrappings from the device and discard them.
- Retrieve all the components from the carton and carefully examine the manual.
- Please pay special attention to operational instructions, cautions, and essential protections to avoid any accidents or damage to property.
- The crisper trays and drawers should be completely rinsed and dried after being cleaned in hot, soapy water. Only the crisper plates and drawers may be placed in the dishwasher.
- To extend the life of the drawers, we suggest hand washing them. NEVER clean the main unit of the dishwasher.

This book contains something for everyone, whether you're just getting started with air frying or an experienced cook looking for some fresh ideas. Each person at the table will be satisfied by the selection, which includes sweets, beverages, and crunchy appetizers. There are numerous delicious breakfast recipes, recipes for crispy chicken and other poultry, juicy lamb and beef, recipes for wholesome vegetables and sides, recipes for fresh fish and other seafood, they are going to blow your mind!

Each recipe includes a thorough list of easily available ingredients and is broken down into clear but understandable steps. Additionally, you are able to spend quality time with best pals and relatives because these recipes are always so simple to prepare, many of which can be prepared in under thirty minutes. With these recipes, you can quickly become captivated with the Ninja Dual Zone Air Fryer and all your greatest culinary desires.

So why are you still waiting? Grab this cookbook, inhale the aroma of mouth watering treats, and leave your taste buds occupied!

Cleaning and Caring for Ninja Foodi 2-Basket Air Fryer

Following each use, you must give the device a thorough cleaning. Whenever you want to clean your device, make sure it is unplugged from the wall.

MAIN UNIT

Use a moist cloth to wash the product and the control panel. WARNING: DO NOT SUBMERGE the product in any kind of liquid. Dishwashers should never be used to clean the main unit.

CRISPER PLATES

Both the dishwasher and manual washing are suitable for crisper plates. You may either let everything dry naturally or dry it with a towel if you wash it by hand.

BASKETS

A dishwasher or hand washing is acceptable for these baskets. Dry all components by either letting them air dry or patting them dry with a towel if you're hand washing them. We advise hand washing your basket to ensure its longevity. Put the plates or baskets from the crisper into a sink full of warm, soapy water to loosen any food particles that may be adhered to them.

Ninja Dual Zone Air Fryer Cooking Tips

If you're using the Ninja Air Fryer for the first time, remember to preheat it for 3 minutes at 200°C to eliminate any manufacturing smells.

For frozen foods, preheat the air fryer for 5 minutes at 199°C to ensure that your food cooks evenly.

After the preheating cycle is completed, add your food to the baskets and ensure the food is not touching the sides of the baskets to avoid uneven cooking.

If you wish the cooking in both compartments to finish at the same time (when foods have different temps, times, or cook functions), select the desired cooking function in Zone 1 and Zone 2, press SYNC, and then press the start button to initiate cooking in the zone with the longest cooking time. The other zone will display Hold, and the unit will beep and activate the second zone when both zones have the same time remaining.

If you wish to cook a larger amount of the same food, put ingredients in the baskets and insert them in both zones. Select the desired cooking function, temperature, and time. Press the MATCH button to copy the zone 1 settings to zone 2. Then Press' start' to begin cooking in both zones.

Remove the food using silicone-tipped tongs or utensils.

Frequency Asked Questions & Notes

How do I change the time or temperature if I only use one zone?

When only one zone is on, the up and down arrows can be used to alter the time or temperature at any time.

How do I change the time or temperature when both zones are in use?

Choose the zone you want, then use the arrows next to TEMP to alter the temperature or the arrows next to TIME to change the time.

How do I take a moment or stop one zone once using both zones?

Choose the zone you want to stop or start playing in, and then press this same START/PAUSE button.

When air-frying, why do some ingredients fly around?

From time to time, the air fryer's fan will move light foods around. Use made of wood toothpicks to keep food like the top bread slice on a sandwich from falling off.

Can I air-fry things that are wet and battered?

Yes, but make sure you use the right breading method. It's essential to coat foods with flour, egg, and bread crumbs in that order. So that crumbs don't get blown away by the fan, press the breading firmly onto the battered items.

What caused a circuit breaker to trip while the unit was being used?

The unit utilizes 1690 watts of electrical power, so it needs to be plugged into a 15-amp outlet. If you plug a plug into a 10-amp breaker, the breaker will trip. When the unit is in use, it is also essential that it is the only thing plugged into an outlet. Make sure the unit is the only thing plugged into an outlet on a 15-amp blocker to avoid tripping a breaker.

Helpful Advice for Ninja dual zone air fryer

Make sure the ingredients are laid out evenly and without overlap on the bottom of the drawer for consistent browning. Make careful to shake the ingredients halfway through the designated cooking time if they are overlapping.

You can alter the cooking temperature and duration at any moment.

Simply choose the zone you wish to change, then use the TEMP or TIME arrows to change the temperature or the time.

Reduce the temperature by 10°C if you're converting recipes from your normal oven.

To prevent overcooking, periodically check your food.

On occasion, the air fryer's fan will fling light meals in all directions.

Secure food with cocktail sticks, such as the top slice of bread on a sandwich, to help with this.

For consistent, crisp results, the crisper plates elevate the ingredients in the drawers so that air can circulate under and around them.

Pressing the dial after choosing a cooking function will start cooking right away. The temperature and time settings on the device will be used.

Use at least 1 tablespoon of oil when cooking fresh veggies and potatoes for the best results. To obtain the required level of crispiness, add extra oil as needed.

For the best outcomes, keep an eye on the food while it cooks and take it out when the required level of brownness has been reached. In order to keep track of the interior temperatures of meat and fish, we advise utilising an instant-read thermometer.

To achieve the greatest results, take food out of the oven as soon as the cooking process is finished.

Chapter 2
Dessert Recipes

Fruity Mini Pies

Prep time: 20 minutes | Cook time: 35 minutes | Serves 2

- 125g plain flour
- ½ teaspoon salt
- 50g shortening
- 60g butter
- 80ml cold water
- For the Fruit Filling
- 1 chopped apple
- 1 tablespoon water
- 1 teaspoon coarse sugar

1. Trace around a 15cm round baking pan on an 20cm x 27.5cm sheet of paper. Remove the circle and set it aside.
2. Combine the flour and salt in a medium mixing bowl. Cut the shortening and butter into pea-size pieces using a pastry blender.
3. One tablespoon of cold water is sprinkled over a portion of the flour mixture. With a fork, toss the ingredients together.
4. Place the moistened pastry on the bowl's side. Continue with the remaining flour. Form a ball with the flour mixture and knead it gently.
5. Flatten the pastry slightly on a lightly floured board, then roll it out into a 32.5cm circle from the centre to edge. Place the pattern near one of the pastry's edges.
6. Cut a 15cm circle of pastry with a small, sharp knife. Make two circles by repeating the process.
7. Half of the Fruit Filling should be placed on half of the pastry circle, leaving a 35cm border. Using water, wet the naked edge.
8. Fold the pastry's empty half over the filling. To seal the pie, use a fork to press around the edge. With a fork, poke a few holes in the top. Rep with the remaining pastry and filling.
9. Combine the egg and water in a small mixing bowl. Brush the tops of the pies with the egg wash, and then sprinkle with the coarse sugar.
10. Press either "Zone 1" or "Zone 2" and then rotate the knob to select "Air Fryer".
11. Set the temperature to 160 degrees C, and then set the time for 5 minutes to preheat.
12. After preheating, place them into the Air Fryer basket.
13. Slide the basket into the Air Fryer and set the time for 35 minutes.
14. After cooking time is completed, transfer onto serving plates and serve.

Chocolate Muffins

Prep time: 15 minutes | Cook time: 15 minutes | Serves 12

- 250g plain flour
- 4 tablespoons cocoa powder
- ½ teaspoon baking soda
- 2 teaspoons baking powder
- ½ teaspoon salt
- 240ml coconut milk
- 100g granulated sugar
- 6 tablespoons coconut oil, melted
- 1 teaspoon vanilla extract
- 170g dark chocolate chips
- 60g pistachios, chopped

1. In a bowl, add the flour, cocoa powder, baking powder, baking soda, and salt and mix well.
2. In another bowl, add the coconut milk, sugar, coconut oil and vanilla extract and beat until well combined.
3. Add the flour mixture and mix until just combined.
4. Fold in the chocolate chips and pistachios.
5. Grease 2 (6-cups) silicone muffin tins.
6. Place the mixture into prepared muffin cups about ¾ full.
7. Press your chosen zone - "Zone 1" or "Zone 2" and then rotate the knob to select "Air Fry".
8. Set the temperature to 150 degrees C and then set the time for 5 minutes to preheat.
9. After preheating, arrange 1 muffin tin into the basket of each zone.
10. Slide the basket into the Air Fryer and set the time for 15 minutes.
11. After cooking time is completed, remove the muffin tin from Air Fryer.
12. Place the muffin molds onto a wire rack to cool for about 10 minutes.
13. Carefully invert the muffins onto the wire rack to completely cool before serving.

Plum Crisp

Prep time: 15 minutes | Cook time: 40 minutes | Serves 4

- 495g plums, pitted and sliced
- 100g sugar, divided
- 3 teaspoons cornflour
- 6 tablespoons flour
- ½ teaspoon ground cinnamon
- Pinch of salt
- 3 tablespoon cold butter, chopped
- 6 tablespoons rolled oats

1. In a bowl, place plum slices, 2 teaspoons of sugar and cornflour and toss to coat well.
2. Divide the plum mixture into 4 lightly greased ramekins.
3. In a bowl, mix together the flour, remaining sugar, cinnamon and salt.
4. With a pastry blender, cut in the butter until a crumbly mixture forms.
5. Add the oats and gently stir to combine.
6. Place the oat mixture over plum slices into each ramekin.
7. Press either "Zone 1" or "Zone 2" and then rotate the knob to select "Bake".
8. Set the temperature to 175 degrees C and then set the time for 5 minutes to preheat.
9. After preheating, arrange ramekins into the basket.
10. Slide basket into Air Fryer and set the time for 40 minutes.
11. After cooking time is completed, remove the ramekins from Air Fryer.
12. Place the ramekins onto a wire rack to cool for about 10 minutes before serving.

Lemon Cheesecake

Prep time: 8 minutes | Cook time: 25 minutes | Serves 2

- 615g ricotta cheese
- 2 eggs
- 1 tablespoon fresh lemon juice
- 3 tablespoons corn flour
- 2 teaspoon vanilla extract
- 1 teaspoon fresh lemon zest, finely grated

1. Press either "Zone 1" or "Zone 2" and then rotate the knob to select "Bake".
2. Set the temperature to 160 degrees C and then set the time for 5 minutes to preheat.
3. Take a bowl, mix together all the ingredients.
4. Place the mixture into a baking dish.
5. After preheating, arrange baking dish into the basket.
6. Slide basket into Air Fryer and set the time for 25 minutes.
7. After cooking time is completed, remove from the Air Fryer.
8. Set aside to cool.
9. Serve and enjoy!

Cinnamon Sugar Dessert Fries

Prep time: 5 minutes | Cook time: 15 minutes | Serves 4

- 2 sweet potatoes
- 1 tablespoon butter, melted
- 1 teaspoon butter, melted
- 2 tablespoons sugar
- ½ teaspoon ground cinnamon

1. Peel and cut the sweet potatoes into skinny fries.
2. Coat the fries with 1 tablespoon of butter.
3. Install a crisper plate into each drawer. Place half the sweet potatoes in the zone 1 drawer and half in zone 2's, then insert the drawers into the unit.
4. Select zone 1, select AIR FRY, set temperature to 390 degrees F/ 200 degrees C, and set time to 15 minutes. Select MATCH to match zone 2 settings to zone 1. Press the START/STOP button to begin cooking.
5. When the time reaches 11 minutes, press START/STOP to pause the unit. Remove the drawers and flip the fries. Re-insert the drawers into the unit and press START/STOP to resume cooking.
6. Meanwhile, mix the 1 teaspoon of butter, the sugar, and the cinnamon in a large bowl.
7. When the fries are done, add them to the bowl, and toss them to coat.
8. Serve and enjoy!

Lava Cake

Prep time: 10 minutes | Cook time: 10 minutes | Serves 4

- 1 cup semi-sweet chocolate chips
- 8 tablespoons butter
- 4 eggs
- 2 teaspoons vanilla extract
- ½ teaspoon salt
- 6 tablespoons all-purpose flour
- 1 cup powdered sugar
- 2 tablespoons Nutella
- 1 tablespoon butter, softened
- 1 tablespoon powdered sugar

1. Heat the chocolate chips and butter in a medium-sized microwave-safe bowl in 30-second intervals until thoroughly melted and smooth, stirring after each interval.
2. Whisk together the eggs, vanilla, salt, flour, and powdered sugar in a mixing bowl.
3. Combine the Nutella, softened butter, and powdered sugar in a separate bowl.
4. Spray 4 ramekins with oil and fill them halfway with the chocolate chip mixture. Fill each ramekin halfway with Nutella, then top with the remaining chocolate chip mixture, making sure the Nutella is well covered.
5. Install a crisper plate in both drawers. Place 2 ramekins in each drawer and insert the drawers into the unit.
6. Select zone 1, select AIR FRY, set temperature to 390 degrees F/ 200 degrees C, and set time to 22 minutes. Select MATCH to match zone 2 settings to zone 1. Press the START/STOP button to begin cooking.
7. Serve hot.

Fruity Oreo Muffins

Prep time: 10 minutes | Cook time: 10 minutes | Serves 3

- 120ml milk
- ½ pack Oreo biscuits, crushed
- ½ teaspoon cocoa powder
- ½ teaspoon baking soda
- ¼ teaspoon baking powder

1. Take a bowl, add milk, cocoa powder, baking soda, biscuits and baking powder. Mix them well.
2. Place the mixture into prepared muffin cups evenly.
3. Line each basket of "Zone 1" and "Zone 2" with parchment paper.
4. Press your chosen zone - "Zone 1" or "Zone 2" and then rotate the knob to select "Air Fry".
5. Set the temperature to 160 degrees C and then set the time for 5 minutes to preheat.
6. After preheating, arrange the muffin cups into the basket.
7. Slide the basket into the Air Fryer and set the time for 10 minutes.
8. After cooking time is completed, remove the muffin cups from Air Fryer.
9. Refrigerate.
10. Serve and enjoy!

Apple Pie Rolls

Prep time: 15 minutes | Cook time: 12 minutes | Serves 8

- 330g tart apples, peeled, cored and chopped
- 110g light brown sugar
- 2½ teaspoon ground cinnamon, divided
- 1 teaspoon corn flour
- 8 egg roll wrappers
- 120g cream cheese, softened
- Non-stick cooking spray
- 2 tablespoons sugar

1. In a small bowl, mix together the apples, brown sugar, 1 teaspoon of cinnamon and corn flour.
2. Arrange 1 egg roll wrapper onto a smooth surface.
3. Spread about 1 tablespoon of cream cheese over roll, leaving 2.5cm of edges.
4. Place ⅓ cup of apple mixture over one corner of a wrapper, just below the centre.
5. Fold the bottom corner over filling.
6. With wet fingers, moisten the remaining wrapper edges.
7. Fold side corners toward centre over the filling.
8. Roll egg roll up tightly and with your fingers, press at tip to seal.
9. Repeat with the remaining wrappers, cream cheese and filling.
10. Spray the rolls with cooking spray evenly.
11. Press your chosen zone - "Zone 1" or "Zone 2" and then rotate the knob to select "Air Fry".
12. Set the temperature to 200 degrees C and then set the time for 5 minutes to preheat.
13. After preheating, arrange 4 rolls into the basket of each zone.
14. Slide the basket into the Air Fryer and set the time for 12 minutes.
15. While cooking, flip the rolls once halfway through and spray with the cooking spray.
16. Meanwhile, in a shallow dish, mix together the sugar and remaining cinnamon.
17. After cooking time is completed, remove the rolls from Air Fryer.
18. Coat the rolls with sugar mixture and serve.

Chocolate Cream Cake

Prep time: 12 minutes | Cook time: 25 minutes | Serves 6

- 3 eggs
- 120g sour cream
- 115g butter, softened
- 2 teaspoon vanilla extract
- 10 tablespoons sugar
- 125g flour
- 1 teaspoon baking powder
- 5 tablespoons cocoa powder
- ½ teaspoon baking soda
- A pinch of salt

1. Take a bowl, add the flour, cocoa powder, baking powder, baking soda and salt. Mix well.
2. Now, add remaining ingredients and whisk well with an electric beater.
3. Place the mixture evenly into a greased cake pan.
4. Press either "Zone 1" and "Zone 2" and then rotate the knob to select "Air Fry".
5. Set the temperature to 160 degrees C and then set the time for 5 minutes to preheat.
6. After preheating, arrange the pan into the basket.
7. Slide basket into Air Fryer and set the time for 25 minutes.
8. After cooking time is completed, remove the pan from Air Fryer.
9. Set aside to cool.
10. Serve and enjoy!

Sweet Dough Dippers

Prep time: 25 minutes | Cook time: 16 minutes | Serves 12

- 455g bread dough, defrosted
- 115g butter, melted
- 200g sugar
- 240g heavy cream
- 300g semi-sweet chocolate chips
- 2 tablespoons Amaretto liqueur

1. Make two 37.5cm logs out of the dough. Each should be cut into 20 segments.
2. Twist the dough halves together 3 to 4 times after cutting each slice.
3. Place the twisted dough on a baking sheet and coat it with melted butter before sprinkling sugar on top.
4. Press your chosen zone - "Zone 1" or "Zone 2" and then rotate the knob to select "Air Fryer".
5. Set the temperature to 175 degrees C, and then set the time for 5 minutes to preheat.
6. After preheating, place into the Air Fryer basket of each zone.
7. Slide the baskets into Air Fryer and set the time for 10 minutes.
8. Make the chocolate amaretto sauce while the dough is cooking. Over medium heat, bring the heavy cream to a simmer.
9. Place the chocolate chips in a large mixing bowl and pour the hot cream over them. Stir constantly until the chocolate begins to melt.
10. After cooking time is completed, transfer onto serving plates and serve with sauce.

Air Fry Brownies

Prep time: 20 minutes | Cook time: 35 minutes | Serves 2

- 60g butter, melted
- 100g sugar
- 1 egg
- ½ teaspoon vanilla extract
- 40g plain flour
- 3 tablespoons unsweetened cocoa
- ⅛ teaspoon baking powder
- ⅛ teaspoon salt

1. Combine melted butter and sugar in a medium mixing bowl. Mix in the egg and vanilla extract thoroughly.
2. Stir in the dry ingredients until barely mixed.
3. Pour batter into the pans that have been prepared.
4. Press either "Zone 1" or "Zone 2" and then rotate the knob to select "Air Fryer".
5. Set the temperature to 165 degrees C, and then set the time for 5 minutes to preheat.
6. After preheating, place pans into the Air Fryer basket of chosen zone.
7. Slide the basket into the Air Fryer and set the time for 13 minutes.
8. After cooking time is completed, transfer onto serving plates and serve.

Speedy Chocolate Espresso Mini Cheesecake

Prep time: 5 minutes | Cook time: 15 minutes | Serves 2

- ½ cup walnuts
- 2 tablespoons salted butter
- 2 tablespoons granular erythritol
- 4 ounces full-fat cream cheese, softened
- 1 large egg
- ½ teaspoon vanilla extract
- 2 tablespoons powdered erythritol
- 2 teaspoons unsweetened cocoa powder
- 1 teaspoon espresso powder

1. Put butter, granular erythritol and walnuts in a food processor. Pulse until all the ingredients stick together to form a dough.
2. Place dough into 4&quot| springform pan and put into the air fryer basket.
3. Set the temperature to 400°F, then set the timer for 5 minutes.
4. When timer goes off, remove crust and allow it to cool.
5. Combine cream cheese with vanilla extract, egg, powdered erythritol, espresso powder and cocoa powder until smooth in a medium bowl.
6. Pour mixture on top of baked walnut crust and put into the air fryer basket.
7. Set the temperature for 300°F, then set the timer for 10 minutes.
8. Once fully cooked, allow to chill for 2 hours before serving.

Jelly Donuts

Prep time: 5 minutes | Cook time: 5 minutes | Serves 4

- 1 package Pillsbury Grands (Homestyle)
- ½ cup seedless raspberry jelly
- 1 tablespoon butter, melted
- ½ cup sugar

1. Install a crisper plate in both drawers. Place half of the biscuits in the zone 1 drawer and half in zone 2's, then insert the drawers into the unit. You may need to cook in batches.
2. Select zone 1, select AIR FRY, set temperature to 390 degrees F/ 200 degrees C, and set time to 22 minutes. Select MATCH to match zone 2 settings to zone 1. Press the START/STOP button to begin cooking.
3. Place the sugar into a wide bowl with a flat bottom.
4. Baste all sides of the cooked biscuits with the melted butter and roll in the sugar to cover completely.
5. Using a long cake tip, pipe 1–2 tablespoons of raspberry jelly into each biscuit. You've now got raspberry-filled donuts!

Citrus Mousse

Prep time: 10 minutes | Cook time: 12 minutes | Serves 4

- 200g cream cheese, softened
- 240g heavy cream
- 4 tablespoons fresh lime juice
- 4 tablespoons maple syrup
- Pinch of salt

1. For mousse: Press either "Zone 1" or "Zone 2" and then rotate the knob to select "Bake".
2. Set the temperature to 175 degrees C and then set the time for 5 minutes to preheat.
3. In a bowl, add all the ingredients and mix until well combined.
4. Transfer the mixture into 4 ramekins.
5. After preheating, arrange ramekins into the basket.
6. Slide basket into Air Fryer and set the time for 12 minutes.
7. After cooking time is completed, remove the ramekins from Air Fryer.
8. Set the ramekins aside to cool.
9. Refrigerate the ramekins for at least 3 hours before serving.

Soft Pecan Brownies

Prep time: 10 minutes | Cook time: 20 minutes | Serves 6

- ½ cup blanched finely ground almond flour
- ½ cup powdered erythritol
- 2 tablespoons unsweetened cocoa powder
- ½ teaspoon baking powder
- ¼ cup unsalted butter, softened
- 1 large egg
- ¼ cup chopped pecans
- ¼ cup low-carb, sugar-free chocolate chips

1. Stir erythritol, almond flour, baking powder and cocoa powder in a large bowl. Add in egg and butter, mix well.
2. Fold in chocolate chips and pecans. Pour mixture into 6&quot| round baking pan. Put pan into the air fryer basket.
3. Set the temperature to 300°F, then set the timer for 20 minutes.
4. A toothpick inserted in center will come out clean when completely cooked. Let it rest for 20 minutes to fully cool and firm up. Serve immediately.

Banana Muffin

Prep time: 10 minutes | Cook time: 25 minutes | Serves 8

- 2 packs banana muffin mix
- 2 eggs, beaten
- 2/3 cup milk

1. Combine ingredients in a bowl.
2. Add to muffin cups.
3. Place muffin cups inside the air fryer basket.
4. Select bake setting.
5. Cook at 320 degrees F for 25 minutes.

Carrot Cake

Prep time: 10 minutes | Cook time: 15 minutes | Serves 6

- 1 carrot cake mix

1. Follow instructions for preparing carrot mix.
2. Pour batter into the air fryer basket.
3. Select air fry function.
4. Cook at 280 degrees F for 15 minutes.

Broiled Grapefruit

Prep time: 5 minutes | Cook time: 5 minutes | Serves 4

- 2 grapefruit, sliced in half
- 2 tablespoons brown sugar

1. Sprinkle grapefruit with sugar.
2. Add to the air fryer basket.
3. Set it to broil.
4. Cook for 5 minutes.

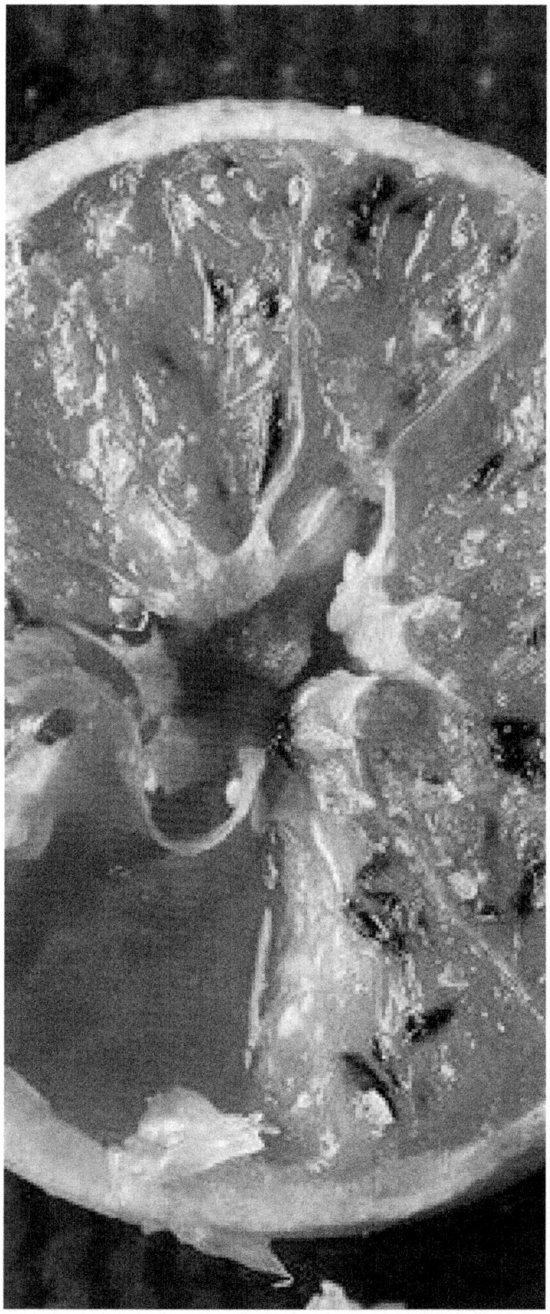

Sweet Protein Powder Doughnut Holes

Prep time: 25 minutes | Cook time: 6 minutes | Serves 6 (2 per serving)

- ½ cup blanched finely ground almond flour
- ½ cup low-carb vanilla protein powder
- ½ cup granular erythritol
- ½ teaspoon baking powder
- 1 large egg
- 5 tablespoons unsalted butter, melted
- ½ teaspoon vanilla extract

1. Stir all ingredients well in a large bowl. Put into the freezer for at least 20 minutes.
2. Wet your hands with water, then form the dough into 12 balls with your hands.
3. Slice a sheet of parchment which fit your air fryer basket. Handling in batches if needed, put doughnut holes into the air fryer basket onto the parchment.
4. Set the temperature to 380°F, then set the timer for 6 minutes.
5. Turn doughnut holes over halfway through the cooking time.
6. Allow them to cool fully before serving.

Semolina Cake

Prep time: 10 minutes | Cook time: 15 minutes | Serves 6

- 335g semolina
- 40g raisins
- 40g walnuts, chopped
- ½ teaspoon baking soda
- 1½ teaspoon baking powder
- 120ml vegetable oil
- 240ml milk
- 240g plain Greek yogurt
- 200g sugar
- A pinch of salt

1. Take a bowl, add the semolina, oil, milk, sugar and yogurt. Mix well.
2. Cover the bowl and set aside for 15 minutes.
3. Add baking soda, baking powder and salt in the semolina mixture. Mix well.
4. Fold in the raisins and walnuts.
5. Press either "Zone 1" or "Zone 2" and then rotate the knob to select "Air Fry".
6. Set the temperature to 160 degrees C and then set the time for 5 minutes to preheat.
7. After preheating, arrange the pan into the basket.
8. Slide basket into Air Fryer and set the time for 15 minutes.
9. After cooking time is completed, remove the pan from Air Fryer.
10. Set aside to cool.
11. Serve and enjoy!

Easy Mini Chocolate Chip Pan Cookie

Prep time: 10 minutes | Cook time: 7 minutes | Serves 4

- ½ cup blanched finely ground almond flour
- ¼ cup powdered erythritol
- 2 tablespoons unsalted butter, softened
- 1 large egg
- ½ teaspoon unflavored gelatin
- ½ teaspoon baking powder
- ½ teaspoon vanilla extract
- 2 tablespoons low-carb, sugar-free chocolate chips

1. Combine erythritol and almond flour in a large bowl. Add in egg, gelatin, and butter , stir well.
2. Stir in vanilla and baking powder and then fold in chocolate chips. Spoon batter into 6&quot| round baking pan. Put pan into the air fryer basket.
3. Set the temperature to 300°F, then set the timer for 7 minutes.
4. The top of the cookie will be golden brown and a toothpick inserted in center will come out clean when fully cooked. Allow to rest for more than 10 minutes.

Oatmeal Cookies

Prep time: 10 minutes | Cook time: 7 minutes |Serves 20

- 200g brown sugar
- 100g granulated sugar
- 230g butter, melted
- 2 large eggs
- 2 teaspoons vanilla extract
- 125g plain flour
- 1 teaspoon baking soda
- 1 teaspoon cinnamon
- ¾ teaspoon salt
- 250g rolled oats

1. In a mixing dish, combine both sugars and melted butter. Blend until everything is well combined.
2. Combine the eggs and vanilla extract in a mixing bowl. Beat the drums thoroughly.
3. Sift the flour, baking soda, cinnamon, and salt over the top and whisk until everything is thoroughly combined.
4. Add the rolled oats and mix well.
5. Line the baskets of your Air Fryer with parchment paper.
6. Press your chosen zone - "Zone 1" or "Zone 2" and then rotate the knob to select "Air Fryer".
7. Set the temperature to 150 degrees C, and then set the time for 5 minutes to preheat.
8. After preheating, fill the Air Fryer basket with walnut-sized cookie dough balls of each zone.
9. Slide the baskets into Air Fryer and set the time for 7 minutes.
10. After cooking time is completed, transfer onto serving plates and serve.

Air Fried Churros

Prep time: 10 minutes | Cook time: 13 minutes | Serves 8

- 180ml plus 2 tablespoons water
- 60g butter
- 1 tablespoon sugar
- Pinch of salt
- 95g flour
- 2 medium eggs
- 100g sugar
- 1 teaspoon cinnamon

1. Bring the water, butter, sugar, and a pinch of salt to a boil in a medium saucepan over medium heat.
2. Reduce the heat to low and quickly stir in the flour with a wooden spatula after the mixture has reached a boil. Stir the mixture continuously until it thickens.
3. Mix everything in a stand mixer bowl.
4. Once the churros dough has cooled slightly, add the eggs one at a time, mixing constantly. Fill a piping bag with the churros mixture.
5. Pipe 7 - 10 cm long churros onto a baking sheet. Using a pair of scissors, cut the end. Freeze the baking sheet for at least 30 minutes.
6. Press your chosen zone - "Zone 1" or "Zone 2" and then rotate the knob to select "Air Fryer".
7. Set the temperature to 180 degrees C, and then set the time for 5 minutes to preheat.
8. After preheating, gently remove the frozen churros from the parchment paper and place them into the air fryer basket of each zone.
9. Slide the baskets into Air Fryer and set the time for 7 minutes.
10. After cooking time is completed, transfer onto serving plates and serve.

Vanilla Soufflé

Prep time: 15 minutes | Cook time: 23 minutes | Serves 6

- 60g butter, softened
- 30g plain flour
- 100g plus 2 tablespoons sugar, divided
- 240ml milk
- 3 teaspoons vanilla extract, divided
- 4 egg yolks
- 5 egg whites
- 1 teaspoon cream of tartar
- 2 tablespoons icing sugar plus extra for dusting

1. In a bowl, add the butter and flour and mix until a smooth paste forms.
2. In a medium pan, mix together 100 g of sugar and milk over medium-low heat and cook for about 3 minutes or until the sugar is dissolved, stirring continuously.
3. Add the flour mixture, whisking continuously and simmer for about 3-4 minutes or until mixture becomes thick.
4. Remove from the heat and stir in 1 teaspoon of vanilla extract.
5. Set aside for about 10 minutes to cool.
6. In a bowl, mix together the egg yolks and 1 teaspoon of vanilla extract.
7. Add the egg yolk mixture into milk mixture and mix until well combined.
8. In another bowl, add the egg whites, cream of tartar, remaining sugar, and vanilla extract and whisk until stiff peaks form.
9. Fold the egg whites mixture into milk mixture.
10. Place the mixture into 6 greased ramekins evenly and with the back of a spoon, smooth the top surface.
11. Press your chosen zone - "Zone 1" or "Zone 2" and then rotate the knob to select "Air Fry".
12. Set the temperature to 165 degrees C and then set the time for 5 minutes to preheat.
13. After preheating, arrange 3 ramekins into the basket of each zone.
14. Slide the basket into the Air Fryer and set the time for 16 minutes.
15. After cooking time is completed, remove the ramekins from Air Fryer.
16. Place the ramekins onto a wire rack to cool slightly.
17. Sprinkle with the icing sugar and serve warm.

Blueberry Cobbler

Prep time: 15 minutes | Cook time: 20 minutes | Serves 12

- For Filling
- 665g fresh blueberries
- 2 teaspoons vanilla extract
- 2 teaspoons fresh lime juice
- 400g sugar
- 2 teaspoons plain flour
- 2 tablespoons butter, melted
- For Topping
- 440g plain flour
- 150g sugar
- 8 teaspoons baking powder
- 480ml milk
- 10 tablespoons butter

1. In a bowl, add all filling ingredients and mix until well combined.
2. For topping: in another large bowl, mix together the flour, baking powder, and sugar.
3. Add the milk and butter and mix until a crumbly mixture forms.
4. In the bottom of 2 greatened baking pans, place the blueberry mixture and top with the flour mixture evenly.
5. Press your chosen zone - "Zone 1" or "Zone 2" and then rotate the knob to select "Air Fry".
6. Set the temperature to 160 degrees C and then set the time for 5 minutes to preheat.
7. After preheating, arrange 1 baking pan into the basket of each zone.
8. Slide the basket into the Air Fryer and set the time for 20 minutes.
9. After cooking time is completed, remove the baking pans from Air Fryer.
10. Place the pans of blueberry cobbler onto a wire rack to cool for about 10 minutes before serving.

Cherry Crumble

Prep time: 15 minutes | Cook time: 25 minutes | Serves 8

- 2 (350g) cans cherry pie filling
- 115g butter, softened
- 125g plus 2 tablespoons self-rising flour
- 150g plus 2 tablespoons caster sugar
- Pinch of salt

1. In 2 lightly greased baking pans, place the cherry pie filling evenly.
2. In a medium bowl, add the remaining ingredients and mix until a crumbly mixture forms.
3. Spread the mixture over cherry pie filling in each pan evenly.
4. Press your chosen zone - "Zone 1" or "Zone 2" and then rotate the knob to select "Air Fry".
5. Set the temperature to 160 degrees C and then set the time for 5 minutes to preheat.
6. After preheating, arrange 1 baking pan into the basket of each zone.
7. Slide the basket into the Air Fryer and set the time for 25 minutes.
8. After cooking time is completed, remove the baking pans from Air Fryer.
9. Place the baking pan onto a wire rack to cool for about 10 minutes before serving.

Chocolate Mug Cakes

Prep time: 15 minutes | Cook time: 17 minutes | Serves 4

- 125g flour
- 8 tablespoons sugar
- 1 teaspoon baking powder
- ½ teaspoon baking soda
- ¼ teaspoon salt
- 8 tablespoons milk
- 8 tablespoons applesauce
- 2 tablespoons vegetable oil
- 1 teaspoon vanilla extract
- 8 tablespoons chocolate chips

1. Press either "Zone 1" or "Zone 2" and then rotate the knob to select "Bake".
2. Set the temperature to 190 degrees C and then set the time for 5 minutes to preheat.
3. In a bowl, mix together the flour, sugar, baking powder, baking soda and salt.
4. Add the milk, applesauce, oil and vanilla extract and mix until well combined.
5. Gently fold in the chocolate chips.
6. Divide the mixture into 4 heatproof mugs.
7. After preheating, arrange 2 mugs into the basket.
8. Slide basket into Air Fryer and set the time for 17 minutes.
9. After cooking time is completed, remove the mugs from Air Fryer.
10. Place the mugs onto a wire rack to cool for about 10 minutes before serving.

Stuffed Apples

Prep time: 15 minutes | Cook time: 10 minutes | Serves 8

- 8 small firm apples, cored
- 160g golden raisins
- 70g blanched almonds
- 4 tablespoons sugar
- ¼ teaspoon ground cinnamon

1. In a food processor, add raisins, almonds, sugar and cinnamon and pulse until chopped.
2. Carefully stuff each apple with raisin mixture.
3. Line each basket of "Zone 1" and "Zone 2" with parchment paper.
4. Press your chosen zone - "Zone 1" or "Zone 2" and then rotate the knob to select "Air Fry".
5. Set the temperature to 180 degrees C and then set the time for 5 minutes to preheat.
6. After preheating, arrange 4 apples into the basket of each zone.
7. Slide the basket into the Air Fryer and set the time for 10 minutes.
8. After cooking time is completed, remove the apples from Air Fryer.
9. Transfer the apples onto plates and set aside to cool slightly before serving.

Chapter 3
Breakfast Recipes

Cornbread

Prep time: 15 minutes | Cook time: 15 minutes | Serves: 6

- 1 cup cornmeal
- 1 cup all-purpose flour
- 1 tablespoon sugar
- 2 teaspoons baking powder
- ½ teaspoon baking soda
- ½ teaspoon salt
- 1 stick butter melted
- 1½ cups buttermilk
- 2 eggs
- 113g diced chiles

1. Mix cornmeal with flour, sugar, baking powder, baking soda, salt, butter, milk, eggs and chiles in a bowl until smooth.
2. Spread this mixture in two greased 4-inch baking pans.
3. Place one pan in each air fryer basket.
4. Return the air fryer basket 1 to Zone 1, and basket 2 to Zone 2 of the Ninja Foodi 2-Basket Air Fryer.
5. Choose the "Air Fry" mode for Zone 1 at 330 degrees F and 15 minutes of cooking time.
6. Select the "MATCH COOK" option to copy the settings for Zone 2.
7. Initiate cooking by pressing the START/PAUSE BUTTON.
8. Slice and serve.

Breakfast Cheese Sandwich

Prep time: 10 minutes | Cook time: 8 minutes | Serves 2

- 4 bread slices
- 2 provolone cheese slice
- ¼ tsp dried basil
- 2 tbsp mayonnaise
- 2 Monterey jack cheese slice
- 2 cheddar cheese slice
- ¼ tsp dried oregano

1. In a small bowl, mix mayonnaise, basil, and oregano.
2. Spread mayonnaise on one side of the two bread slices.
3. Top two bread slices with cheddar cheese, provolone cheese, Monterey jack cheese slice, and cover with remaining bread slices.
4. Insert a crisper plate in the Ninja Foodi air fryer baskets.
5. Place sandwiches in both baskets.
6. Select zone 1, then select "air fry" mode and set the temperature to 390 degrees F for 8 minutes. Press "match" to match zone 2 settings to zone 1. Press "start/stop" to begin. Turn halfway through.

Cheesy Baked Eggs

Prep time: 10 minutes | Cook time: 16 minutes | Serves: 4

- 4 large eggs
- 57g smoked gouda, shredded
- Everything bagel seasoning, to taste
- Salt and pepper to taste

1. Crack one egg in each ramekin.
2. Top the egg with bagel seasoning, black pepper, salt and gouda.
3. Place 2 ramekins in each air fryer basket.
4. Return the air fryer basket 1 to Zone 1, and basket 2 to Zone 2 of the Ninja Foodi 2-Basket Air Fryer.
5. Choose the "Air Fry" mode for Zone 1 and set the temperature to 400 degrees F and 16 minutes of cooking time.
6. Select the "MATCH COOK" option to copy the settings for Zone 2.
7. Initiate cooking by pressing the START/PAUSE BUTTON.
8. Serve warm.

Apple Fritters

Prep time: 15 minutes | Cook time: 7 minutes | Serves 4

- 2 apples, cored and diced
- 1 cup all-purpose flour
- 2 tablespoons sugar
- 1 teaspoon baking powder
- ½ teaspoon salt
- ½ teaspoon ground cinnamon
- ¼ teaspoon ground nutmeg
- 79ml milk
- 2 tablespoons butter, melted
- 1 egg
- ½ teaspoon lemon juice
- Cinnamon Glaze
- ½ cup confectioners' sugar
- 2 tablespoons milk
- ½ teaspoons ground cinnamon
- Pinch of salt

1. Mix flour, sugar and the rest of the batter ingredients in a bowl until smooth.
2. Fold in apples and mix evenly.
3. Layer the two air fryer baskets with parchment paper.
4. Drop the batter spoon by spoon into the baskets with a 1-inch gap between each fritter.
5. Return the air fryer basket 1 to Zone 1, and basket 2 to Zone 2 of the Ninja Foodi 2-Basket Air Fryer.
6. Choose the "Air Fry" mode for Zone 1 at 370 degrees F and 7 minutes of cooking time.
7. Select the "MATCH COOK" option to copy the settings for Zone 2.
8. Initiate cooking by pressing the START/PAUSE BUTTON.
9. Meanwhile, mix salt, cinnamon, milk, and sugar in a bowl.
10. Serve the fritters with the glaze on top.

Breakfast Frittata

Prep time: 10 minutes | Cook time: 12 minutes | Serves 4

- 4 eggs
- 4 tablespoons milk
- 35g cheddar cheese grated
- 50g feta crumbled
- 1 tomato, deseeded and chopped
- 15g spinach chopped
- 1 tablespoon fresh herbs, chopped
- 2 spring onion chopped
- Salt and black pepper, to taste
- ½ teaspoon olive oil

1. Beat eggs with milk in a bowl and stir in the rest of the ingredients.
2. Grease two small-sized springform pans and line them with parchment paper.
3. Divide the egg mixture into the pans and place one in each air fryer basket.
4. Return the air fryer basket 1 to Zone 1, and basket 2 to Zone 2 of the Ninja Foodi 2-Basket Air Fryer.
5. Choose the "Air Fry" mode for Zone 1 at 350 degrees F and 12 minutes of cooking time.
6. Select the "MATCH COOK" option to copy the settings for Zone 2.
7. Initiate cooking by pressing the START/PAUSE BUTTON.
8. Serve warm.

Sweet Potato Hash

Prep time: 10 minutes | Cook time: 15 minutes | Serves 4

- 3 sweet potatoes, peel & cut into ½-inch pieces
- ½ tsp cinnamon
- 2 tbsp olive oil
- 1 bell pepper, cut into ½-inch pieces
- ½ tsp dried thyme
- ½ tsp nutmeg
- 1 medium onion, cut into ½-inch pieces
- Pepper
- Salt

1. In a bowl, toss sweet potatoes with the remaining ingredients.
2. Insert a crisper plate in Ninja Foodi air fryer baskets.
3. Add potato mixture in both baskets.
4. Select zone 1 then select "air fry" mode and set the temperature to 355 degrees F for 15 minutes. Press "match" to match zone 2 settings to zone 1. Press "start/stop" to begin.

Jelly Doughnuts

Prep time: 10 minutes | Cook time: 16 minutes | Serves: 4

- 1 package Pillsbury Grands
- ½ cup seedless raspberry jelly
- 1 tablespoon butter, melted
- ½ cup sugar

1. Spread the Pillsbury dough and cut out 3 inches round doughnuts out of it.
2. Place the doughnuts in the air fryer baskets and brush them with butter.
3. Drizzle sugar over the doughnuts.
4. Return the air fryer basket 1 to Zone 1, and basket 2 to Zone 2 of the Ninja Foodi 2-Basket Air Fryer.
5. Choose the "Air Fry" mode for Zone 1 at 320 degrees F and 6 minutes of cooking time.
6. Select the "MATCH COOK" option to copy the settings for Zone 2.
7. Initiate cooking by pressing the START/PAUSE BUTTON.
8. Use a piping bag to inject raspberry jelly into each doughnut.
9. Serve.

Air Fried Bacon and Eggs

Prep time: 5 minutes | Cook time: 10 minutes | Serves 1

- 2 eggs
- 2 slices bacon

1. Grease a ramekin using cooking spray.
2. Install the crisper plate in the zone 1 drawer and place the bacon inside it. Insert the drawer into the unit.
3. Crack the eggs and add them to the greased ramekin.
4. Install the crisper plate in the zone 2 drawer and place the ramekin inside it. Insert the drawer into the unit.
5. Select zone 1 to AIR FRY for 9–11 minutes at 400 degrees F/ 200 degrees C. Select zone 2 to AIR FRY for 8–9 minutes at 350 degrees F/ 175 degrees C. Press SYNC.
6. Press START/STOP to begin cooking.
7. Enjoy!

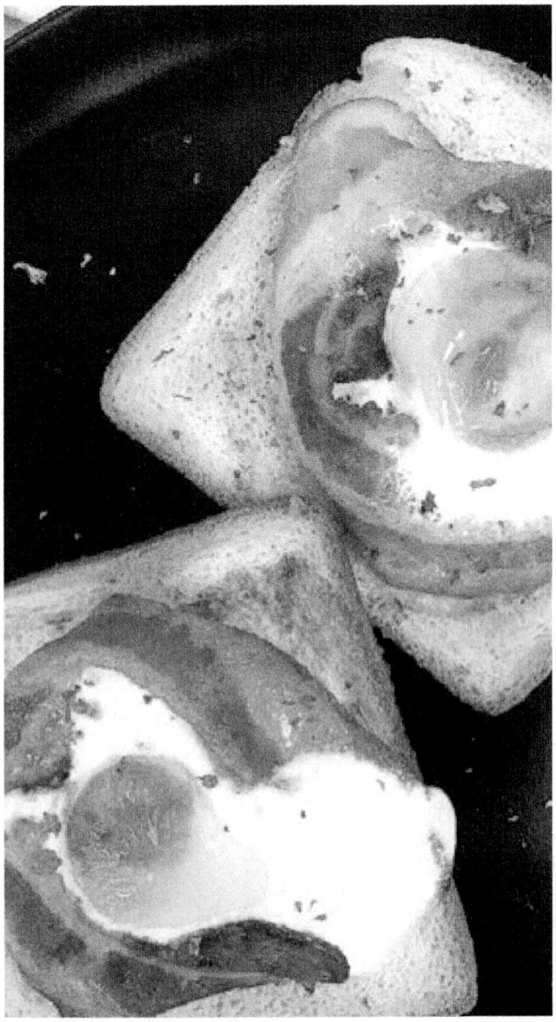

Brussels Sprouts Potato Hash

Prep time: 15 minutes | Cook time: 10 minutes | Serves 4

- 455g Brussels sprouts
- 1 small to medium red onion
- 227g baby red potatoes
- 2 tablespoons avocado oil
- ½ teaspoon salt
- ½ teaspoon black pepper

1. Peel and boil potatoes in salted water for 15 minutes until soft.
2. Drain and allow them to cool down then dice.
3. Shred Brussels sprouts and toss them with potatoes and the rest of the ingredients.
4. Divide this veggies hash mixture in both of the air fryer baskets.
5. Return the air fryer basket 1 to Zone 1, and basket 2 to Zone 2 of the Ninja Foodi 2-Basket Air Fryer.
6. Choose the "Air Fry" mode for Zone 1 with 375 degrees F temperature and 10 minutes of cooking time.
7. Select the "MATCH COOK" option to copy the settings for Zone 2.
8. Initiate cooking by pressing the START/PAUSE BUTTON.
9. Shake the veggies once cooked halfway through.
10. Serve warm.

Sweet Potato Sausage Hash

Prep time: 10 minutes | Cook time: 20 minutes | Serves 4

- 1½ pounds sweet potato, peeled and diced into ½-inch pieces
- 1 tablespoon minced garlic
- 1 teaspoon kosher salt plus more, as desired
- Ground black pepper, as desired
- 2 tablespoons canola oil
- 1 tablespoon dried sage
- 1-pound uncooked mild ground breakfast sausage
- ½ large onion, peeled and diced
- ½ teaspoon ground cinnamon
- 1 teaspoon chili powder
- 4 large eggs, poached or fried (optional)

1. Toss the sweet potatoes with the garlic, salt, pepper, and canola oil in a mixing bowl.
2. Install the crisper plate in the zone 1 drawer, fill it with the sweet potato mixture, and insert the drawer in the unit.
3. Place the ground sausage in the zone 2 drawer (without the crisper plate) and place it in the unit.
4. Select zone 1, then AIR FRY, and set the temperature to 400 degrees F/ 200 degrees C with a 30-minute timer.
5. Select zone 2, then ROAST, then set the temperature to 400 degrees F/ 200 degrees C with a 20-minute timer. SYNC is the option to choose. To begin cooking, press the START/STOP button.
6. When the zone 1 and zone 2 times have reached 10 minutes, press START/STOP and remove the drawers from the unit. Shake each for 10 seconds.
7. Half of the sage should be added to the zone 1 drawer.
8. Add the onion to the zone 2 drawer and mix to incorporate. To continue cooking, press START/ STOP and reinsert the drawers.
9. Remove both drawers from the unit once the cooking is finished and add the potatoes to the sausage mixture. Mix in the cinnamon, sage, chili powder, and salt until thoroughly combined.
10. When the hash is done, stir it and serve it right away with a poached or fried egg on top, if desired.

Turkey Ham Muffins

Prep time: 10 minutes | Cook time: 10 minutes | Serves: 16

- 1 egg
- 340g all-purpose flour
- 85g turkey ham, chopped
- 2 tbsp mix herbs, chopped
- 235g cheddar cheese, shredded
- 1 onion, chopped
- 2 tsp baking powder
- 2 tbsp butter, melted
- 237ml milk
- Pepper
- Salt

1. In a large bowl, mix flour and baking powder.
2. Add egg, butter, and milk and mix until well combined.
3. Add herbs, cheese, onion, and turkey ham and mix well.
4. Insert a crisper plate in the Ninja Foodi air fryer baskets.
5. Pour the batter into the silicone muffin moulds.
6. Place muffin moulds in both baskets.
7. Select zone 1, then select "air fry" mode and set the temperature to 355 degrees F for 10 minutes. Press "match" to match zone 2 settings to zone 1. Press "start/stop" to begin.

Sausage Breakfast Casserole

Prep time: 10 minutes | Cook time: 10 minutes | Serves: 4

- 455g hash browns
- 455g ground breakfast sausage
- 1 green capsicum diced
- 1 red capsicum diced
- 1 yellow capsicum diced
- ¼ cup sweet onion diced
- 4 eggs

1. Layer each air fryer basket with parchment paper.
2. Place the hash browns in both the baskets.
3. Spread sausage, onion and peppers over the hash brown.
4. Return the air fryer basket 1 to Zone 1, and basket 2 to Zone 2 of the Ninja Foodi 2-Basket Air Fryer.
5. Choose the "Air Fry" mode for Zone 1 at 355 degrees F temperature and 10 minutes of cooking time.
6. Select the "MATCH COOK" option to copy the settings for Zone 2.
7. Initiate cooking by pressing the START/PAUSE BUTTON.
8. Beat eggs in a bowl and pour over the air fried veggies.
9. Continue air frying for 10 minutes.
10. Garnish with salt and black pepper.
11. Serve warm.

Healthy Oatmeal Muffins

Prep time: 10 minutes | Cook time: 17 minutes | Serves 6

- 1 egg
- ¼ tsp ground ginger
- 1 tsp ground cinnamon
- ½ tsp baking soda
- ½ tsp baking powder
- 55g brown sugar
- ½ tsp vanilla
- 2 tbsp butter, melted
- 125g applesauce
- 61ml milk
- 68gm whole wheat flour
- 100gm quick oats
- Pinch of salt

1. In a mixing bowl, mix together all dry the ingredients.
2. In a separate bowl, add the remaining ingredients and mix well.
3. Add the dry ingredients mixture into the wet mixture and mix until well combined.
4. Pour the batter into the silicone muffin moulds.
5. Insert a crisper plate in the Ninja Foodi air fryer baskets.
6. Place muffin moulds in both baskets.
7. Select zone 1 then select "bake" mode and set the temperature to 390 degrees F for 17 minutes. Press "start/stop" to begin.

Wholemeal Blueberry Muffins

Prep time: 10 minutes | Cook time: 15 minutes | Serves 6

- Olive oil cooking spray
- 120 ml unsweetened applesauce
- 60 ml honey
- 120 ml non-fat plain Greek yoghurt
- 1 teaspoon vanilla extract
- 1 large egg
- 350 ml plus 1 tablespoon wholemeal, divided
- ½ teaspoon baking soda
- ½ teaspoon baking powder
- ½ teaspoon salt
- 120 ml blueberries, fresh or frozen

1. Lightly coat the inside of six silicone muffin cups or a six-cup muffin tin with olive oil cooking spray.
2. In a large bowl, combine the applesauce, honey, yoghurt, vanilla, and egg and mix until smooth. Sift in 350 ml of the flour, the baking soda, baking powder, and salt into the wet mixture, then stir until just combined. In a small bowl, toss the blueberries with the remaining 1 tablespoon flour, then fold the mixture into the muffin batter.
3. Divide the mixture evenly among the prepared muffin cups and place into the zone 1 drawer of the air fryer. Bake at 182°C for 12 to 15 minutes, or until golden brown on top and a toothpick inserted into the middle of one of the muffins comes out clean. Allow to cool for 5 minutes before serving.

Breakfast Casserole

Prep time: 5 minutes | Cook time: 10 minutes | Serves 4

- 1 pound beef sausage, grounded
- ¼ cup diced white onion
- 1 diced green bell pepper
- 8 whole eggs, beaten
- ½ cup Colby Jack cheese, shredded
- ¼ teaspoon garlic salt
- Oil spray, for greasing

1. Take a bowl and add the grounded sausage to it.
2. Add in the diced onions, bell peppers, eggs and whisk it well.
3. Then season it with garlic salt.
4. Spray both the baskets of the air fryer with oil spray.
5. Divide this mixture among the baskets; remember to remove the crisper plates.
6. Top the mixture with cheese.
7. Now, turn ON the Ninja Foodie 2-Basket Air Fryer zone 1 and select AIR FRY mode and set the time to 10 minutes at 390 degrees F/ 200 degrees C.
8. Select the MATCH button for zone 2 baskets, and hit START/STOP button.
9. Once the cooking cycle is complete, take out, and serve.
10. Serve and enjoy.

Sausage with Eggs

Prep time: 10 minutes | Cook time: 13 minutes | Serves 2

- 4 sausage links, raw and uncooked
- 4 eggs, uncooked
- 1 tablespoon green onion
- 2 tablespoons chopped tomatoes
- Salt and black pepper, to taste
- 2 tablespoons milk, dairy
- Oil spray, for greasing

1. Take a bowl and whisk eggs in it.
2. Then pour milk, and add the onions and tomatoes.
3. Whisk it all well.
4. Now season it with salt and black pepper.
5. Take one cake pan that fits inside the air fryer and grease it with oil spray.
6. Pour the omelet into the greased cake pan.
7. Put the cake pan inside zone 1 of the Ninja Foodie 2-Basket Air Fryer.
8. Now place the sausage link into the zone 2 basket.
9. Select BAKE for zone 1 basket and set the timer to 8-10 minutes at 300 degrees F/ 150 degrees C.
10. For zone 2, select the AIR FRY button and set the timer to 12 minutes at 390 degrees F/ 200 degrees C.
11. Once the cooking cycle is complete, serve by transferring it to plates.
12. Chop the sausage or cut it in round chunks and then mix it with the egg.
13. Enjoy hot as a delicious breakfast.

Cinnamon Toasts

Prep time: 15 minutes | Cook time: 8 minutes | Serves 4

- 4 pieces of bread
- 2 tablespoons butter
- 2 eggs, beaten
- 1 pinch salt
- 1 pinch cinnamon ground
- 1 pinch nutmeg ground
- 1 pinch ground clove
- 1 teaspoon icing sugar

1. Add two eggs to a mixing bowl and stir cinnamon, nutmeg, ground cloves, and salt, then whisk well.
2. Spread butter on both sides of the bread slices and cut them into thick strips.
3. Dip the breadsticks in the egg mixture and place them in the two crisper plates.
4. Return the crisper plates to the Ninja Foodi Dual Zone Air Fryer.
5. Choose the Air Fry mode for Zone 1 and set the temperature to 390 degrees F/ 200 degrees C and the time to 8 minutes.
6. Select the "MATCH" button to copy the settings for Zone 2.
7. Initiate cooking by pressing the START/STOP button.
8. Flip the French toast sticks when cooked halfway through.
9. Serve.

Honey-Apricot Granola with Greek Yoghurt

Prep time: 10 minutes | Cook time: 30 minutes | Serves 6

- 235 ml rolled oats
- 60 ml dried apricots, diced
- 60 ml almond slivers
- 60 ml walnuts, chopped
- 60 ml pumpkin seeds
- 60 to 80 ml honey, plus more for drizzling
- 1 tablespoon olive oil
- 1 teaspoon ground cinnamon
- ¼ teaspoon ground nutmeg
- ¼ teaspoon salt
- 2 tablespoons sugar-free dark chocolate chips (optional)
- 700 ml fat-free plain Greek yoghurt

1. Line the zone 1 and zone 2 drawer with two parchment papers. In a large bowl, combine the oats, apricots, almonds, walnuts, pumpkin seeds, honey, olive oil, cinnamon, nutmeg, and salt, mixing so that the honey, oil, and spices are well distributed. Pour the mixture onto the parchment papers and spread it into an even layer.
2. Bake at 130°C for 10 minutes, then shake or stir and spread back out into an even layer. Continue baking for 10 minutes more, then repeat the process of shaking or stirring the mixture.
3. Bake for an additional 10 minutes before removing from the air fryer. Allow the granola to cool completely before stirring in the chocolate chips (if using) and pouring into an airtight container for storage. For each serving, top 120 ml Greek yoghurt with 80 ml granola and a drizzle of honey, if needed.

Easy Pancake Doughnuts

Prep time: 10 minutes | Cook time: 9 minutes | Serves 8

- 2 eggs
- 50g sugar
- 125ml vegetable oil
- 240g pancake mix
- 1 ½ tbsp cinnamon

1. In a bowl, mix pancake mix, eggs, cinnamon, sugar, and oil until well combined.
2. Pour the doughnut mixture into the silicone doughnut moulds.
3. Insert a crisper plate in Ninja Foodi air fryer baskets.
4. Place doughnut moulds in both baskets.
5. Select zone 1 then select "air fry" mode and set the temperature to 355 degrees F for 9 minutes. Press "match" to match zone 2 settings to zone 1. Press "start/stop" to begin.

Air Fryer Sausage Patties

Prep time: 5 minutes | Cook time: 10 minutes | Serves 12

- 1-pound pork sausage or ready-made patties
- Fennel seeds or preferred seasonings

1. Prepare the sausage by slicing it into patties, then flavor it with fennel seed or your favorite seasonings.
2. Install a crisper plate in both drawers. Place half the patties in zone 1 and half in zone 2, then insert the drawers into the unit.
3. Select zone 1, select AIR FRY, set temperature to 390 degrees F/ 200 degrees C, and set time to 10 minutes.
4. Select MATCH to match zone 2 settings to zone 1.
5. Press the START/STOP button to begin cooking.
6. When cooking is complete, remove the patties from the unit and serve with sauce or make a burger.

Roasted Oranges

Prep time: 15 minutes | Cook time: 6 minutes | Serves 4

- 2 oranges, halved
- 2 teaspoons honey
- 1 teaspoon cinnamon

1. Place the oranges in each air fryer basket.
2. Drizzle honey and cinnamon over the orange halves.
3. Return the air fryer basket 1 to Zone 1, and basket 2 to Zone 2 of the Ninja Foodi 2-Basket Air Fryer.
4. Choose the "Air Fry" mode for Zone 1 at 395 degrees F temperature and 6 minutes of cooking time.
5. Select the "MATCH COOK" option to copy the settings for Zone 2.
6. Initiate cooking by pressing the START/PAUSE BUTTON.
7. Serve.

Cinnamon Apple French Toast

Prep time: 10 minutes | Cook time: 10 minutes | Serves: 8

- 1 egg, lightly beaten
- 4 bread slices
- 1 tbsp cinnamon
- 15ml milk
- 23ml maple syrup
- 45 ml applesauce

1. In a bowl, whisk egg, milk, cinnamon, applesauce, and maple syrup.
2. Insert a crisper plate in the Ninja Foodi air fryer baskets.
3. Dip each slice in egg mixture and place in both baskets.
4. Select zone 1 then select "air fry" mode and set the temperature to 355 degrees F for 10 minutes. Press "match" to match zone 2 settings to zone 1. Press "start/stop" to begin.

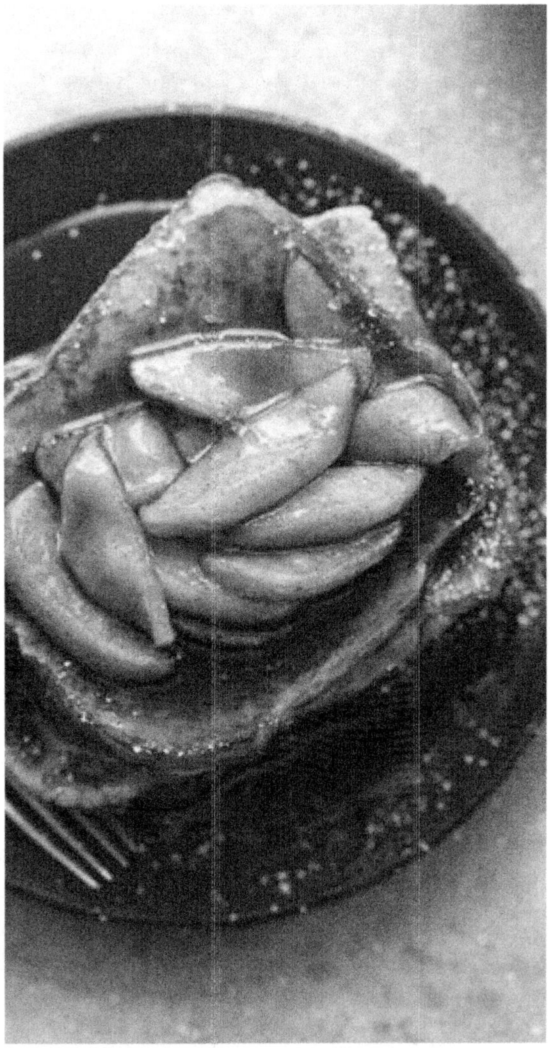

Wholemeal Banana-Walnut Bread

Prep time: 10 minutes | Cook time: 23 minutes | Serves 6

- Olive oil cooking spray
- 2 ripe medium bananas
- 1 large egg
- 60 ml non-fat plain Greek yoghurt
- 60 ml olive oil
- ½ teaspoon vanilla extract
- 2 tablespoons honey
- 235 ml wholemeal flour
- ¼ teaspoon salt
- ¼ teaspoon baking soda
- ½ teaspoon ground cinnamon
- 60 ml chopped walnuts

1. Lightly coat the inside of two 5 ½-by-3-inch loaf pans with olive oil cooking spray.
2. In a large bowl, mash the bananas with a fork. Add the egg, yoghurt, olive oil, vanilla, and honey. Mix until well combined and mostly smooth. Sift the wholemeal flour, salt, baking soda, and cinnamon into the wet mixture, then stir until just combined. Do not overmix. Gently fold in the walnuts. Pour into the prepared loaf pans and spread to distribute evenly.
3. Place a loaf pan in the zone 1 drawer and another pan into zone 2 drawer. In zone 1, select Bake button and adjust temperature to 180°C, set time to 20 to 23 minutes. In zone 2, select Match Cook and press Start.
4. Remove until golden brown on top and a toothpick inserted into the center comes out clean. Allow to cool for 5 minutes before serving.

Breakfast Stuffed Peppers

Prep time: 10 minutes | Cook time: 13 minutes | Serves 4

- 2 capsicums, halved, seeds removed
- 4 eggs
- 1 teaspoon olive oil
- 1 pinch salt and pepper
- 1 pinch sriracha flakes

1. Cut each capsicum in half and place two halves in each air fryer basket.
2. Crack one egg into each capsicum and top it with black pepper, salt, sriracha flakes and olive oil.
3. Return the air fryer basket 1 to Zone 1, and basket 2 to Zone 2 of the Ninja Foodi 2-Basket Air Fryer.
4. Choose the "Air Fry" mode for Zone 1 at 390 degrees F and 13 minutes of cooking time.
5. Select the "MATCH COOK" option to copy the settings for Zone 2.
6. Initiate cooking by pressing the START/PAUSE BUTTON.
7. Serve warm.

Breakfast Potatoes

Prep time: 15 minutes | Cook time: 20 minutes | Serves 6

- 3 potatoes, peeled and diced
- 1 onion yellow, diced
- 1 green pepper diced
- 2 teaspoons salt
- ½ teaspoon pepper
- 2 tablespoons olive oil
- 1 cup cheese shredded

1. Toss potatoes with onion, green peppers, black pepper, salt and cheese in a bowl.
2. Divide the potato mixture into the Ninja Foodi 2 Baskets Air Fryer baskets.
3. Return the air fryer basket 1 to Zone 1, and basket 2 to Zone 2 of the Ninja Foodi 2-Basket Air Fryer.
4. Choose the "Air Fry" mode for Zone 1 at 400 degrees F temperature and 20 minutes of cooking time.
5. Select the "MATCH COOK" option to copy the settings for Zone 2.
6. Initiate cooking by pressing the START/PAUSE BUTTON.
7. Toss the veggies once cooked halfway through.
8. Serve warm.

Honey Banana Oatmeal

Prep time: 10 minutes | Cook time: 8 minutes | Serves 4

- 2 eggs
- 2 tbsp honey
- 1 tsp vanilla
- 45g quick oats
- 73ml milk
- 30g Greek yoghurt
- 219g banana, mashed

1. In a bowl, mix eggs, milk, yoghurt, honey, vanilla, oats, and mashed banana until well combined.
2. Pour batter into the four greased ramekins.
3. Insert a crisper plate in the Ninja Foodi air fryer baskets.
4. Place ramekins in both baskets.
5. Select zone 1 then select "air fry" mode and set the temperature to 390 degrees F for 8 minutes. Press "match" to match zone 2 settings to zone 1. Press "start/stop" to begin.

Vanilla Strawberry Doughnuts

Prep time: 10 minutes | Cook time: 15 minutes | Serves 8

- 1 egg
- ½ cup strawberries, diced
- 80ml cup milk
- 1 tsp cinnamon
- 1 tsp baking soda
- 136g all-purpose flour
- 2 tsp vanilla
- 2 tbsp butter, melted
- 73g sugar
- ½ tsp salt

1. In a bowl, mix flour, cinnamon, baking soda, sugar, and salt.
2. In a separate bowl, whisk egg, milk, butter, and vanilla.
3. Pour egg mixture into the flour mixture and mix until well combined.
4. Add strawberries and mix well.
5. Pour batter into the silicone doughnut moulds.
6. Insert a crisper plate in the Ninja Foodi air fryer baskets.
7. Place doughnut moulds in both baskets.
8. Select zone 1, then select "air fry" mode and set the temperature to 320 degrees F for 15 minutes. Press "match" to match zone 2 settings to zone 1. Press "start/stop" to begin.

Sausage & Butternut Squash

Prep time: 10 minutes | Cook time: 20 minutes | Serves 2

- 450g butternut squash, diced
- 70g kielbasa, diced
- ¼ onion, diced
- ¼ tsp garlic powder
- ½ tbsp olive oil
- Pepper
- Salt

1. In a bowl, toss butternut squash with garlic powder, oil, onion, kielbasa, pepper, and salt.
2. Insert a crisper plate in the Ninja Foodi air fryer baskets.
3. Add sausage and butternut squash mixture in both baskets.
4. Select zone 1, then select "air fry" mode and set the temperature to 375 degrees F for 20 minutes. Press "match" to match zone 2 settings to zone 1. Press "start/stop" to begin. Stir halfway through.

Quiche Breakfast Peppers

Prep time: 10 minutes | Cook time: 15 minutes | Serves 4

- 4 eggs
- ½ tsp garlic powder
- 112g mozzarella cheese, shredded
- 125g ricotta cheese
- 2 bell peppers, cut in half & remove seeds
- 7½g baby spinach, chopped
- 22g parmesan cheese, grated
- ¼ tsp dried parsley

1. In a bowl, whisk eggs, ricotta cheese, garlic powder, parsley, cheese, and spinach.
2. Pour the egg mixture into each bell pepper half and top with mozzarella cheese.
3. Insert a crisper plate in the Ninja Foodi air fryer baskets.
4. Place bell peppers in both the baskets.
5. Select zone 1 then select "air fry" mode and set the temperature to 355 degrees F for 15 minutes. Press "match" to match zone 2 settings to zone 1. Press "start/stop" to begin.

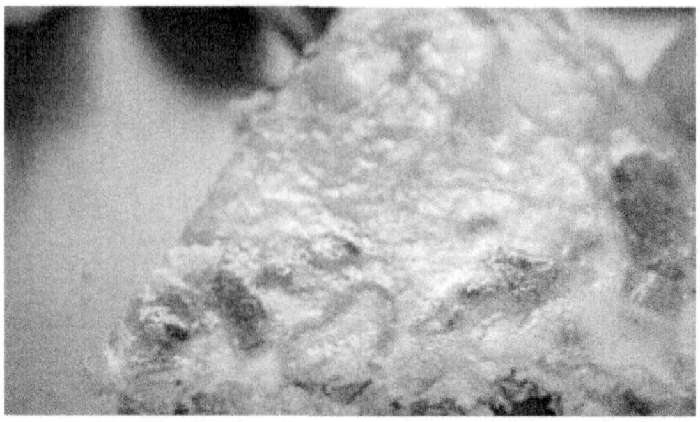

Chapter 4
Poultry Mains Recipes

Herbed Cornish Game Hen

Prep time: 15 minutes | Cook time: 20 minutes | Serves 4

- ¼ cup olive oil
- 1 teaspoon fresh rosemary, chopped
- 1 teaspoon fresh thyme, chopped
- 1 teaspoon fresh lemon zest, finely grated
- ¼ teaspoon sugar
- ¼ teaspoon red pepper flakes, crushed
- Salt and ground black pepper, as required
- 2 pounds Cornish game hen, backbone removed and halved

1. In a large bowl, mix together oil, herbs, lemon zest, sugar, and spices.
2. Add the hen portions and coat with the marinade generously.
3. Cover the bowl and refrigerate for about 24 hours.
4. Arrange a large strainer over a sink.
5. Remove the hen portions from bowl and place into a strainer to drain any liquid.
6. Grease each basket of "Zone 1" and "Zone 2" of Ninja Foodi 2-Basket Air Fryer.
7. Press "Zone 1" and "Zone 2" and then rotate the knob for each zone to select "Air Fry".
8. Set the temperature to 390 degrees F/ 200 degrees C for both zones and then set the time for 5 minutes to preheat.
9. After preheating, arrange 1 hen portion into the basket of each zone.
10. Slide each basket into Air Fryer and set the time for 20 minutes.
11. After cooking time is completed, remove the hen portions from Air Fryer.
12. Cut each portion into half and serve hot.

Spicy Roasted Chicken

Prep time: 15 Minutes | Cook time: 1 hour 10 minutes | Serves 12

- ½ cup butter, softened
- 4 teaspoons dried rosemary
- 4 teaspoons dried thyme
- 2 tablespoons Cajun seasoning
- 2 tablespoons onion powder
- 2 tablespoons garlic powder
- 2 tablespoons paprika
- 2 teaspoons cayenne pepper
- Salt, as required
- 2 (3-pound) whole chicken, neck and giblets removed

1. In a bowl, add the butter, herbs, spices and salt and mix well.
2. Rub each chicken with spice mixture generously.
3. With kitchen twine, tie off the wings and legs of each chicken.
4. Grease each basket of "Zone 1" and "Zone 2" of Ninja Foodi 2-Basket Air Fryer.
5. Press "Zone 1" and "Zone 2" and then rotate the knob for each zone to select "Bake".
6. Set the temperature to 360 degrees F/ 180 degrees C for both zones and then set the time for 5 minutes to preheat.
7. After preheating, arrange 1 chicken into the basket of each zone.
8. Slide each basket into Air Fryer and set the time for 70 minutes.
9. After cooking time is completed, remove the chickens from Air Fryer and place each onto a platter for about 10 minutes before serving.
10. Cut each chicken into desired-sized pieces and serve.

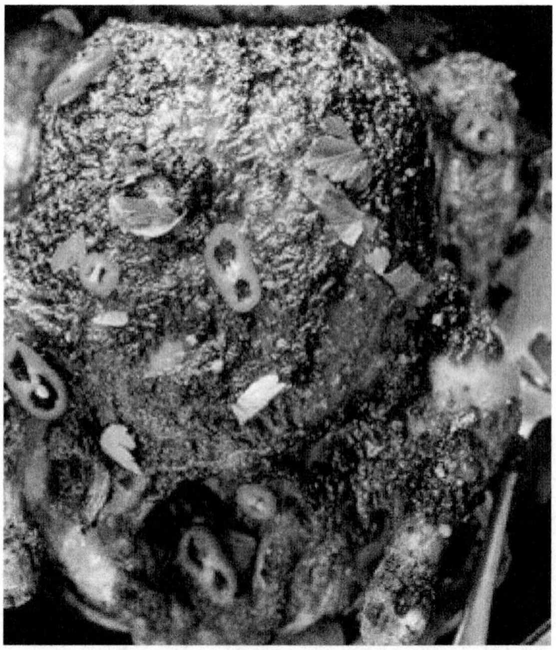

Gingered Chicken Drumsticks

Prep time: 10 minutes, | Cook time: 25 minutes | Serves 6

- ½ cup full-fat coconut milk
- 4 teaspoons fresh ginger, minced
- 4 teaspoons galangal, minced
- 2 teaspoons ground turmeric
- Salt, as required
- 6 (6-ounce) chicken drumsticks

1. In a large bowl, place the coconut milk, galangal, ginger, and spices and mix well.
2. Add the chicken drumsticks and coat with the marinade generously.
3. Refrigerate to marinate for at least 6-8 hours.
4. Grease each basket of "Zone 1" and "Zone 2" of Ninja Foodi 2-Basket Air Fryer.
5. Press "Zone 1" and "Zone 2" and then rotate the knob for each zone to select "Air Fry".
6. Set the temperature to 375 degrees F/ 190 degrees C for both zones and then set the time for 5 minutes to preheat.
7. After preheating, arrange 3 drumsticks into the basket of each zone.
8. Slide each basket into Air Fryer and set the time for 25 minutes.
9. After cooking time is completed, remove the drumsticks from Air Fryer and serve hot.

Roasted Chicken Thighs

Prep time: 10 minutes | Cook time: 20 minutes | Serves 4

- 4 (2-ounce) skinless, boneless chicken thighs
- 2 tablespoons butter, melted
- Salt and ground black pepper, as required

1. Line each basket of "Zone 1" and "Zone 2" of Ninja Foodi 2-Basket Air Fryer with a lightly greased square piece of foil.
2. Press "Zone 1" and "Zone 2" and then rotate the knob for each zone to select "Roast".
3. Set the temperature to 450 degrees F/ 230 degrees C for both zones and then set the time for 5 minutes to preheat.
4. Meanwhile, rub the chicken thighs with salt and black pepper evenly and then brush with melted butter.
5. After preheating, arrange chicken thighs into the basket of each zone.
6. Slide each basket into Air Fryer and set the time for 20 minutes.
7. After cooking time is completed, remove the chicken thighs from Air Fryer.
8. Serve hot.

Juicy Chicken Thighs

Prep time: 10 minutes | Cook time: 20 minutes | Serves 4

- 4 (2½-ounce) chicken thighs
- 1 teaspoon ground cumin
- 1 teaspoon garlic powder
- 1 tablespoon olive oil
- ½ teaspoon smoked paprika
- ½ teaspoon ground coriander
- Salt and ground black pepper, as required

1. In a large bowl, add the spices, salt and black pepper and mix well.
2. Coat the chicken thighs with oil and then rub with spice mixture.
3. Grease each basket of "Zone 1" and "Zone 2" of Ninja Foodi 2-Basket Air Fryer.
4. Press "Zone 1" and "Zone 2" and then rotate the knob for each zone to select "Air Fry".
5. Set the temperature to 400 degrees F/ 200 degrees C for both zones and then set the time for 5 minutes to preheat.
6. After preheating, arrange the chicken thighs into the basket of each zone.
7. Slide each basket into Air Fryer and set the time for 20 minutes.
8. While cooking, flip the chicken thighs once halfway through.
9. After cooking time is completed, remove the chicken thighs from Air Fryer and serve hot.

Spicy Chicken Thighs

Prep time: 10 minutes | Cook time: 20 minutes | Serves 8

- 2 teaspoons ground cumin
- 2 teaspoons garlic powder
- 1 teaspoon smoked paprika
- 1 teaspoon ground coriander
- Salt and ground black pepper, as required
- 8 (5-ounce) chicken thighs
- 4 tablespoons olive oil

1. In a large bowl, add the spices, salt and black pepper and mix well.
2. Coat the chicken thighs with oil and then rub with spice mixture.
3. Grease each basket of "Zone 1" and "Zone 2" of Ninja Foodi 2-Basket Air Fryer.
4. Press "Zone 1" and "Zone 2" and then rotate the knob for each zone to select "Air Fry".
5. Set the temperature to 400 degrees F/ 200 degrees C for both zones and then set the time for 5 minutes to preheat.
6. After preheating, arrange 4 chicken thighs into the basket of each zone.
7. Slide each basket into Air Fryer and set the time for 20 minutes.
8. While cooking, flip the chicken thighs once halfway through.
9. After cooking time is completed, remove the chicken thighs from Air Fryer and serve hot.

Turkey Meatloaf with Veggie Medley

Prep time: 15 minutes |Cook time: 30 minutes | Serves 4

- FOR THE MEATLOAF
- 1 large egg
- ¼ cup ketchup
- 2 teaspoons Worcestershire sauce
- ½ cup Italian-style bread crumbs
- 1 teaspoon kosher salt
- 1 pound ground turkey (93 percent lean)
- 1 tablespoon vegetable oil
- FOR THE VEGGIE MEDLEY
- 2 carrots, thinly sliced
- 8 ounces green beans, trimmed (about 2 cups)
- 2 cups broccoli florets
- 1 red bell pepper, sliced into strips
- 2 tablespoons vegetable oil
- ½ teaspoon kosher salt
- ½ teaspoon freshly ground black pepper

TO PREP THE MEATLOAF:

1. In a large bowl, whisk the egg. Stir in the ketchup, Worcestershire sauce, bread crumbs, and salt. Let sit for 5 minutes to allow the bread crumbs to absorb some moisture.
2. Gently mix in the turkey until just incorporated. Form the mixture into a loaf. Brush with the oil. To prep the veggie medley: In a large bowl, combine the carrots, green beans, broccoli, bell pepper, oil, salt, and black pepper. Mix well to coat the vegetables with the oil. To cook the meatloaf and veggie medley:

1. Install a crisper plate in each of the two baskets. Place the meatloaf in the Zone 1 basket and insert the basket in the unit. Place the vegetables in the Zone 2 basket and insert the basket in the unit.
2. Select Zone 1, select ROAST, set the temperature to 350°F, and set the time to 30 minutes.
3. Select Zone 2, select AIR FRY, set the temperature to 390°F, and set the time to 20 minutes. Select SMART FINISH.
4. Press START/PAUSE to begin cooking.
5. When cooking is complete, the meatloaf will be cooked through (an instant-read thermometer should read165°F) and the vegetables will be tender and roasted.

Crispy Chicken Legs

Prep time: 15 minutes | Cook time: 20 minutes | Serves 6

- 2 cups milk
- 2 cups flour
- 2 teaspoons garlic powder
- 2 teaspoons onion powder
- 2 teaspoons ground cumin
- 2 teaspoons paprika
- Salt and ground black pepper, as required
- 6 (8-ounce) chicken legs

1. In a shallow bowl, place the milk.
2. In another shallow bowl, mix together the flour and spices.
3. Dip the chicken legs into milk and then coat with the flour mixture.
4. Repeat this process once again.
5. Grease each basket of "Zone 1" and "Zone 2" of Ninja Foodi 2-Basket Air Fryer.
6. Press "Zone 1" and "Zone 2" and then rotate the knob for each zone to select "Air Fry".
7. Set the temperature to 360 degrees F/ 180 degrees C for both zones and then set the time for 5 minutes to preheat.
8. After preheating, arrange 2 chicken legs into the basket of each zone.
9. Slide each basket into Air Fryer and set the time for 25 minutes.
10. After cooking time is completed, remove the chicken legs from Air Fryer and serve hot.

Chicken Potatoes

Prep time: 10 minutes | Cook time: 22 minutes | Serves 4

- 15 ounces canned potatoes drained
- 1 teaspoon olive oil
- 1 teaspoon Lawry's seasoned salt
- ⅛ teaspoons black pepper optional
- 8 ounces boneless chicken breast cubed
- ¼ teaspoon paprika
- ⅜ cup cheddar, shredded
- 4 bacon slices, cooked, cut into strips

1. Dice the chicken into small pieces and toss them with olive oil and spices.
2. Drain and dice the potato pieces into smaller cubes.
3. Add potato to the chicken and mix well to coat.
4. Spread the mixture in the two crisper plates in a single layer.
5. Return the crisper plates to the Ninja Foodi Dual Zone Air Fryer.
6. Choose the Air Fry mode for Zone 1 and set the temperature to 390 degrees F/ 200 degrees C and the time to 22 minutes.
7. Select the "MATCH" button to copy the settings for Zone 2.
8. Initiate cooking by pressing the START/STOP button.
9. Top the chicken and potatoes with cheese and bacon.
10. Return the crisper plates to the Ninja Foodi Dual Zone Air Fryer.
11. Select the Max Crisp mode for Zone 1 and set the temperature to 300 degrees F/ 150 degrees C and the time to 5 minutes.
12. Initiate cooking by pressing the START/STOP button.
13. Repeat the same step for Zone 2 to broil the potatoes and chicken in the right drawer.
14. Enjoy with dried herbs on top.

Chili Chicken Wings

Prep time: 20 minutes | Cook time: 43 minutes | Serves 4

- 8 chicken wings drumettes
- cooking spray
- ⅛ cup low-fat buttermilk
- ¼ cup almond flour
- McCormick Chicken Seasoning to taste
- Thai Chili Marinade
- 1½ tablespoons low-sodium soy sauce
- ½ teaspoon ginger, minced
- 1½ garlic cloves
- 1 green onion
- ½ teaspoon rice wine vinegar
- ½ tablespoon Sriracha sauce
- ½ tablespoon sesame oil

1. Put all the ingredients for the marinade in the blender and blend them for 1 minute.
2. Keep this marinade aside. Pat dry the washed chicken and place it in the Ziploc bag.
3. Add buttermilk, chicken seasoning, and zip the bag.
4. Shake the bag well, then refrigerator for 30 minutes for marination.
5. Remove the chicken drumettes from the marinade, then dredge them through dry flour.
6. Spread the drumettes in the two crisper plate and spray them with cooking oil.
7. Return the crisper plate to the Ninja Foodi Dual Zone Air Fryer.
8. Choose the Air Fry mode for Zone 1 and set the temperature to 390 degrees F/ 200 degrees C and the time to 43 minutes.
9. Select the "MATCH" button to copy the settings for Zone 2.
10. Initiate cooking by pressing the START/STOP button.
11. Toss the drumettes once cooked halfway through.
12. Now brush the chicken pieces with Thai chili sauce and then resume cooking.
13. Serve warm.

Lemon Feta Chicken

Prep time: 15 minutes | Cook time: 25 minutes |Serves 2

- 2 chicken breast halves, boneless and skinless
- 2 tablespoons crumbled feta cheese
- ½ teaspoon dried oregano
- ¼ teaspoon pepper
- 2 tablespoons lemon juice

1. Take a baking dish, place chicken and pour lemon juice over chicken.
2. Sprinkle with feta cheese, oregano and pepper.
3. Press "Zone 1" of Ninja Foodi 2-Basket Air Fryer and then rotate the knob for each zone to select "Air Fry".
4. Set the heat to 200 degrees C and then set the time for 5 minutes to preheat.
5. After preheating, arrange chicken into the basket of each zone.
6. Slide the basket into the Air Fryer and set the time for 20 to 25 minutes.
7. After cooking time is completed, remove the chicken breast from Air Fryer.
8. Serve and enjoy.

Air-Fried Turkey Breast with Roasted Green Bean Casserole

Prep time: 10 minutes, plus 15 minutes to rest |Cook time: 50 minutes | Serves 4

- FOR THE TURKEY BREAST
- 2 teaspoons unsalted butter, at room temperature
- 1 bone-in split turkey breast (3 pounds), thawed if frozen
- 1 teaspoon poultry seasoning
- ½ teaspoon kosher salt
- ⅓ teaspoon freshly ground black pepper
- FOR THE GREEN BEAN CASSEROLE
- 1 (10.5-ounce) can condensed cream of mushroom soup
- ½ cup whole milk
- 1 cup store-bought crispy fried onions, divided
- ¼ teaspoon kosher salt
- ¼ teaspoon freshly ground black pepper
- 1 pound green beans, trimmed
- ¼ cup panko bread crumbs
- Nonstick cooking spray

- To prep the turkey breast: Spread the butter over the skin side of the turkey. Season with the poultry seasoning, salt, and black pepper.
- To prep the green bean casserole: In a medium bowl, combine the soup, milk, ½ cup of crispy onions, the salt, and black pepper.

TO COOK THE TURKEY AND BEANS:

1. Install a crisper plate in the Zone 1 basket. Place the turkey skin-side up in the basket and insert the basket in the unit. Place the green beans in the Zone 2 basket and insert the basket in the unit.
2. Select Zone 1, select AIR FRY, set the temperature to 360°F, and set the time to 50 minutes.
3. Select Zone 2, select ROAST, set the temperature to 350°F, and set the time to 40 minutes. Select SMART FINISH.
4. Press START/PAUSE to begin cooking.
5. When the Zone 2 timer reads 30 minutes, press START/PAUSE. Remove the basket and stir the soup mixture into the beans. Scatter the panko and remaining ½ cup of crispy onions over the top, then spritz with cooking spray. Reinsert the basket and press START/PAUSE to resume cooking.
6. When cooking is complete, the turkey will be cooked through (an instant-read thermometer should read 165°F) and the green bean casserole will be bubbling and golden brown on top.
7. Let the turkey and casserole rest for at least 15 minutes before serving.

Cheesy Chicken Breasts

Prep time: 10 minutes | Cook time: 20 minutes | Serves 4

- 2 boneless skinless chicken breast halves
- 2 eggs
- ¼ teaspoon pepper
- 1 cup shredded mozzarella cheese
- 1 cup pasta sauce
- ½ cup breadcrumbs
- ½ cup grated Parmesan cheese

1. In a shallow bowl, beat eggs.
2. Take another bowl, add breadcrumbs, Parmesan cheese and pepper.
3. Dip chicken breast in egg and then coat with breadcrumbs mixture.
4. Grease each basket of "Zone 1" and "Zone 2" of Ninja Foodi 2-Basket Air Fryer.
5. Press "Zone 1" and "Zone 2" and then rotate the knob for each zone to select "Air Fry".
6. Set the heat to 375 degrees F/ 190 degrees C for both zones and then set the time for 5 minutes to preheat.
7. After preheating, arrange chicken thighs into the basket of each zone.
8. Slide each basket into Air Fryer and set the time for 10 to 12 minutes.
9. While cooking, flip the chicken once halfway through and top with sauce and cheese.
10. After cooking time is completed, remove the chicken breast from Air Fryer and serve hot.

Seasoned Chicken Legs

Prep time: 12 minutes | Cook time: 20 minutes | Serves 2

- 2 tablespoons plain Greek yogurt
- ½ teaspoon red chili powder
- ½ teaspoon ground cumin
- ½ teaspoon ground coriander
- 2 (4-ounce) chicken legs
- 1 tablespoon balsamic vinegar
- 1 teaspoon garlic, minced
- Salt, as required
- Ground black pepper, as required

1. In a bowl, add the chicken legs, vinegar, garlic and salt and mix well.
2. Set aside for about 12 minutes.
3. Meanwhile, in another bowl, mix together the yogurt, spices, salt and pepper.
4. Add the chicken legs into the bowl and coat with the spice mixture generously.
5. Cover the bowl of chicken and refrigerate for at least 10-12 hours.
6. Grease each basket of "Zone 1" and "Zone 2" of Ninja Foodi 2-Basket Air Fryer.
7. Press "Zone 1" and "Zone 2" and then rotate the knob for each zone to select "Air Fry".
8. Set the temperature to 400 degrees F/ 200 degrees C for both zones and then set the time for 5 minutes to preheat.
9. After preheating, arrange chicken legs into the basket of each zone.
10. Slide each basket into Air Fryer and set the time for 20 minutes.
11. After cooking time is completed, remove the chicken legs from Air Fryer and serve hot.

Ranch Turkey Tenders with Roasted Vegetable Salad

Prep time: 15 minutes |Cook time: 20 minutes | Serves 4

- FOR THE TURKEY TENDERS
- 1 pound turkey tenderloin
- ¼ cup ranch dressing
- ½ cup panko bread crumbs
- Nonstick cooking spray
- FOR THE VEGETABLE SALAD
- 1 large sweet potato, peeled and diced
- 1 zucchini, diced
- 1 red bell pepper, diced
- 1 small red onion, sliced
- 1 tablespoon vegetable oil
- ¼ teaspoon kosher salt
- ½ teaspoon freshly ground black pepper
- 2 cups baby spinach
- ½ cup store-bought balsamic vinaigrette
- ¼ cup chopped walnuts

- To prep the turkey tenders: Slice the turkey crosswise into 16 strips. Brush both sides of each strip with ranch dressing, then coat with the panko. Press the bread crumbs into the turkey to help them adhere. Mist both sides of the strips with cooking spray.
- To prep the vegetables: In a large bowl, combine the sweet potato, zucchini, bell pepper, onion, and vegetable oil. Stir well to coat the vegetables. Season with the salt and black pepper.

TO COOK THE TURKEY AND VEGETABLES:

1. Install a crisper plate in the Zone 1 basket. Place the turkey tenders in the basket in a single layer and insert the basket in the unit. Place the vegetables in the Zone 2 basket and insert the basket in the unit.
2. Select Zone 1, select AIR FRY, set the temperature to 375°F, and set the time to 20 minutes.
3. Select Zone 2, select ROAST, set the temperature to 400°F, and set the time to 20 minutes. Select SMART FINISH.
4. Press START/PAUSE to begin cooking.
5. When both timers read 10 minutes, press START/PAUSE. Remove the Zone 1 basket and use silicone-tipped tongs to flip the turkey tenders. Reinsert the basket in the unit. Remove the Zone 2 basket and shake to redistribute the vegetables. Reinsert the basket and press START/PAUSE to resume cooking.
6. When cooking is complete, the turkey will be golden brown and cooked through (an instant-read thermometer should read 165°F) and the vegetables will be fork-tender.
7. Place the spinach in a large serving bowl. Mix in the roasted vegetables and balsamic vinaigrette. Sprinkle with walnuts. Serve warm with the turkey tenders.

Simple Turkey Breast

Prep time: 10 minutes | Cook time: 20 minutes |Serves 12

- 2 (1.2kg) bone-in, skin-on turkey breast half
- Salt and ground black pepper, as required

1. Rub the turkey breast with the salt and black pepper evenly.
2. Grease basket of Ninja Foodi 2-Basket Air Fryer.
3. Press your chosen zone - "Zone 1" or "Zone 2" and then rotate the knob to select "Bake".
4. Set the temperature to 200 degrees C and then set the time for 5 minutes to preheat.
5. After preheating, arrange 1 turkey breast into the basket of each zone.
6. Slide the basket into the Air Fryer and set the time for 80 minutes.
7. After cooking time is completed, remove the turkey breasts from Air Fryer and place onto a platter.
8. With a piece of foil, cover each turkey breast for about 20 minutes before slicing.
9. With a sharp knife, cut each turkey breast into desired size slices and serve.

Air Fried Turkey Breast

Prep time: 10 minutes | Cook time: 46 minutes | Serves 4

- 2 lbs. turkey breast, on the bone with skin
- ½ tablespoon olive oil
- 1 teaspoon salt
- ¼ tablespoon dry poultry seasoning

1. Rub turkey breast with ½ tablespoons of oil.
2. Season both its sides with turkey seasoning and salt, then rub in the brush half tablespoons of oil over the skin of the turkey.
3. Divide the turkey in half and place each half in each of the crisper plate.
4. Return the crisper plate to the Ninja Foodi Dual Zone Air Fryer.
5. Choose the Air Fry mode for Zone 1 and set the temperature to 390 degrees F/ 200 degrees C and the time to 46 minutes.
6. Select the "MATCH" button to copy the settings for Zone 2.
7. Initiate cooking by pressing the START/STOP button.
8. Flip the turkey once cooked halfway through, and resume cooking.
9. Slice and serve warm.

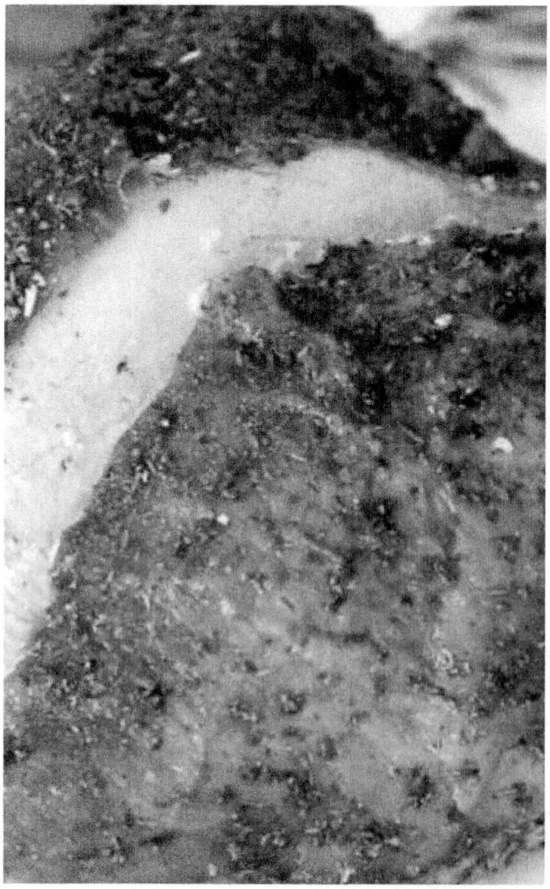

Marinated Chicken Legs

Prep time: 15 minutes | Cook time: 20 minutes | Serves 4

- 4 (8-ounce) chicken legs
- 2 tablespoons balsamic vinegar
- 2 teaspoons garlic, minced
- Salt, as required
- 4 tablespoons plain Greek yogurt
- 1 teaspoon red chili powder
- 1 teaspoon ground cumin
- 1 teaspoon ground coriander
- Ground black pepper, as required

1. In a bowl, add the chicken legs, vinegar, garlic and salt and mix well.
2. Set aside for about 15 minutes.
3. Meanwhile, in another bowl, mix together the yogurt, spices, salt and black pepper.
4. Add the chicken legs into the bowl and coat with the spice mixture generously.
5. Cover the bowl of chicken and refrigerate for at least 10-12 hours.
6. Grease each basket of "Zone 1" and "Zone 2" of Ninja Foodi 2-Basket Air Fryer.
7. Press "Zone 1" and "Zone 2" and then rotate the knob for each zone to select "Air Fry".
8. Set the temperature to 400 degrees F/ 200 degrees C for both zones and then set the time for 5 minutes to preheat.
9. After preheating, arrange 2 chicken legs into the basket of each zone.
10. Slide each basket into Air Fryer and set the time for 20 minutes.
11. After cooking time is completed, remove the chicken legs from Air Fryer and serve hot.

Roasted Chicken

Prep time: 12 minutes | Cook time: 1 hour and 10 minutes | Serves 6

- 1 tablespoon garlic powder
- 1 tablespoon paprika
- 1 teaspoon cayenne pepper
- ¼ cup butter, softened
- 2 teaspoons dried rosemary
- 2 teaspoons dried thyme
- 1 tablespoon Cajun seasoning
- 1 tablespoon onion powder
- 1 (1½-pound) whole chicken, neck and giblets removed
- Salt, as required

1. In a bowl, add the butter, herbs, spices and salt and mix well.
2. Rub each chicken with spice mixture generously.
3. With kitchen twine, tie off the wings and legs of each chicken.
4. Grease each basket of "Zone 1" and "Zone 2" of Ninja Foodi 2-Basket Air Fryer.
5. Press "Zone 1" and "Zone 2" and then rotate the knob for each zone to select "Bake".
6. Set the temperature to 360 degrees F/ 180 degrees C for both zones and then set the time for 5 minutes to preheat.
7. After preheating, arrange the chicken into the basket of each zone.
8. Slide each basket into Air Fryer and set the time for 70 minutes.
9. After cooking time is completed, remove the chickens from Air Fryer and place each onto a platter for about 10 minutes before carving.
10. Cut each chicken into desired-sized pieces and serve.

Simple Chicken Thighs

Prep time: 10 minutes | Cook time: 20 minutes |Serves 8

- 8 (100g) skinless, boneless chicken thighs
- Salt and ground black pepper, as required
- 4 tablespoons butter, melted

1. Line each basket of "Zone 1" and "Zone 2" of Ninja Foodi 2-Basket Air Fryer with a lightly greased square piece of foil.
2. Press your chosen zone - "Zone 1" or "Zone 2" and then rotate the knob to select "Roast".
3. Set the temperature to 230 degrees C and then set the time for 5 minutes to preheat.
4. Meanwhile, rub the chicken thighs with salt and black pepper evenly and then brush with melted butter.
5. After preheating, arrange 4 chicken thighs into the basket of each zone.
6. Slide the basket into the Air Fryer and set the time for 20 minutes.
7. After cooking time is completed, remove the chicken thighs from Air Fryer.
8. Serve hot.

Gingered Chicken Legs

Prep time: 10 minutes | Cook time: 25 minutes | Serves 3

- 3 (3-ounce) chicken legs
- 1 teaspoon ground turmeric
- ¼ cup full-fat coconut milk
- 2 teaspoons fresh ginger, minced
- 2 teaspoons galangal, minced
- Salt, as required

1. In a large bowl, place the coconut milk, galangal, ginger, and spices and mix well.
2. Add the chicken legs and coat with the marinade generously.
3. Refrigerate to marinate for at least 6-8 hours.
4. Grease each basket of "Zone 1" and "Zone 2" of Ninja Foodi 2-Basket Air Fryer.
5. Press "Zone 1" and "Zone 2" and then rotate the knob for each zone to select "Air Fry".
6. Set the temperature to 375 degrees F/ 190 degrees C for both zones and then set the time for 5 minutes to preheat.
7. After preheating, arrange chicken legs into the basket of each zone.
8. Slide each basket into Air Fryer and set the time for 25 minutes.
9. After cooking time is completed, remove the legs from Air Fryer and serve hot.

Glazed Chicken Drumsticks

Prep time: 10 minutes | Cook time: 20 minutes | Serves 4

- ¼ cup Dijon mustard
- 1 tablespoon honey
- 2 tablespoons canola oil
- 1 tablespoon fresh parsley, minced
- Salt and ground black pepper, as required
- 4 (6-ounce) chicken drumsticks

1. In a bowl, add all ingredients except the drumsticks and mix until well combined.
2. Add the drumsticks and coat with the mixture generously.
3. Cover the bowl and place in the refrigerator to marinate overnight.
4. Grease each basket of "Zone 1" and "Zone 2" of Ninja Foodi 2-Basket Air Fryer.
5. Press "Zone 1" and "Zone 2" and then rotate the knob for each zone to select "Air Fry".
6. Set the temperature to 320 degrees F/ 160 degrees C for both zones and then set the time for 5 minutes to preheat.
7. After preheating, arrange 2 drumsticks into the basket of each zone.
8. Slide each basket into Air Fryer and set the time for 12 minutes.
9. After 12 minutes, flip the drumsticks and set the temperature to 390 degrees F/ 200 degrees C for both zones.
10. Set the time for 8 minutes.
11. After cooking time is completed, remove the drumsticks from Air Fryer and serve hot.

Crispy Chicken Drumsticks

Prep time: 15 minutes | Cook time: 25 minutes | Serves 3

- 3 (4-ounce) chicken drumsticks
- 1 teaspoon onion powder
- 1 teaspoon ground cumin
- 1 teaspoon paprika
- 1 cup milk
- 1 cup flour
- 1 teaspoon garlic powder
- Salt and ground black pepper, as required

1. In a shallow bowl, place the milk.
2. In another shallow bowl, mix together the flour and spices.
3. Dip the chicken drumsticks into milk and then coat with the flour mixture.
4. Repeat this process once again.
5. Grease each basket of "Zone 1" and "Zone 2" of Ninja Foodi 2-Basket Air Fryer.
6. Press "Zone 1" and "Zone 2" and then rotate the knob for each zone to select "Air Fry".
7. Set the temperature to 360 degrees F/ 180 degrees C for both zones and then set the time for 5 minutes to preheat.
8. After preheating, arrange chicken drumsticks into the basket of each zone.
9. Slide each basket into Air Fryer and set the time for 25 minutes.
10. After cooking time is completed, remove the chicken drumsticks from Air Fryer and serve hot.

Baked Chicken Breasts

Prep time: 15 minutes | Cook time: 40 minutes | Serves 3

- 3 (2½-ounce) boneless, skinless chicken breasts
- ¼ cup fresh cilantro, chopped
- 1 cup croutons, crushed
- ¼ cup flour
- 1 large egg, beaten

1. In a shallow, dish place the flour.
2. In a second shallows dish, mix together the egg and cilantro.
3. In a third shallow dish, place croutons.
4. Coat the chicken breasts with flour, then dip into eggs and finally coat with croutons.
5. Grease each basket of "Zone 1" and "Zone 2" of Ninja Foodi 2-Basket Air Fryer.
6. Press "Zone 1" and "Zone 2" and then rotate the knob for each zone to select "Bake".
7. Set the temperature to 375 degrees F/ 190 degrees C for both zones and then set the time for 5 minutes to preheat.
8. After preheating, arrange the chicken breasts into the basket of each zone.
9. Slide each basket into Air Fryer and set the time for 40 minutes.
10. While cooking, flip the chicken breasts once halfway through.
11. After cooking time is completed, remove the chicken breasts from Air Fryer
12. Serve hot.

Chapter 5
Beef, Pork, and Lamb

Italian-Style Meatballs with Garlicky Roasted Broccoli

Prep time: 20 minutes | Cook time: 15 minutes | Serves 4

- For the meatballs
- 1 large egg
- ¼ cup Italian-style bread crumbs
- 1 pound ground beef (85 percent lean)
- ¼ cup grated Parmesan cheese
- ¼ teaspoon kosher salt
- Nonstick cooking spray
- 2 cups marinara sauce
- For the roasted broccoli
- 4 cups broccoli florets
- 1 tablespoon olive oil
- ¼ teaspoon kosher salt
- ¼ teaspoon freshly ground pepper
- ¼ teaspoon red pepper flakes
- 1 tablespoon minced garlic

1. To prep the meatballs: In a large bowl, beat the egg. Mix in the bread crumbs and let sit for 5 minutes.
2. Add the beef, Parmesan, and salt and mix until just combined. Form the meatball mixture into 8 meatballs, about 1 inch in diameter. Mist with cooking spray.
3. To prep the broccoli: In a large bowl, combine the broccoli, olive oil, salt, black pepper, and red pepper flakes. Toss to coat the broccoli evenly.
4. To cook the meatballs and broccoli: Install a crisper plate in the Zone 1 basket. Place the meatballs in the basket and insert the basket in the unit. Place the broccoli in the Zone 2 basket, sprinkle the garlic over the broccoli, and insert the basket in the unit.
5. Select Zone 1, select AIR FRY, set the temperature to 400°F, and set the time to 12 minutes.
6. Select Zone 2, select ROAST, set the temperature to 390°F, and set the time to 15 minutes. Select SMART FINISH.
7. Press START/PAUSE to begin cooking.
8. When the Zone 1 timer reads 5 minutes, press START/PAUSE. Remove the basket and pour the marinara sauce over the meatballs. Reinsert the basket and press START/PAUSE to resume cooking.
9. When cooking is complete, the meatballs should be cooked through and the broccoli will have begun to brown on the edges.

Balsamic Steak Tips with Roasted Asparagus and Mushroom Medley

Prep time: 10 minutes | Cook time: 25 minutes | Serves 4

- For the steak tips
- 1½ pounds sirloin tips
- ½ cup olive oil
- ¼ cup balsamic vinegar
- ¼ cup packed light brown sugar
- 1 tablespoon reduced-sodium soy sauce
- 1 teaspoon finely chopped fresh rosemary
- 1 teaspoon minced garlic
- For the asparagus and mushrooms
- 6 ounces sliced cremini mushrooms
- 1 small red onion, sliced
- 1 tablespoon olive oil
- 1 pound asparagus, tough ends trimmed
- ⅛ teaspoon kosher salt

1. To prep the steak tips: In a large bowl, combine the sirloin tips, oil, vinegar, brown sugar, soy sauce, rosemary, and garlic. Mix well to coat the steak.
2. To prep the mushrooms: In a large bowl, combine the mushrooms, onion, and oil.
3. To cook the steak and vegetables: Install a crisper plate in each of the two baskets. Shake any excess marinade from the steak tips, place the steak in the Zone 1 basket, and insert the basket in the unit. Place the mushrooms and onions in the Zone 2 basket and insert the basket in the unit.
4. Select Zone 1, select AIR FRY, set the temperature to 400°F, and set the time to 12 minutes.
5. Select Zone 2, select ROAST, set the temperature to 400°F, and set the time to 25 minutes. Select SMART FINISH.
6. Press START/PAUSE to begin cooking.
7. When the Zone 2 timer reads 10 minutes, press START/PAUSE. Remove the basket, add the asparagus to the mushrooms and onion, and sprinkle with salt. Reinsert the basket and press START/PAUSE to resume cooking.
8. When cooking is complete, the beef should be cooked to your liking and the asparagus crisp-tender. Serve warm.

Strip Steaks with Hasselback Potatoes

Prep time: 15 minutes, plus 5 minutes to rest | Cook time: 30 minutes | Serves 4

- For the strip steak
- 2 boneless strip steaks (8 ounces each)
- 2 teaspoons vegetable oil
- 1 tablespoon steak seasoning
- For the hasselback potatoes
- 4 russet potatoes
- 1 tablespoon vegetable oil
- 1 teaspoon kosher salt
- 1 tablespoon salted butter, at room temperature
- 2 teaspoons minced garlic
- 2 teaspoons minced fresh parsley

1. To prep the strip steak: Brush both sides of the steaks with the oil and season with the steak seasoning.
2. To prep the Hasselback potatoes: Set a potato on a work surface and lay the handles of two wooden spoons lengthwise on either side of the potato. Make crosswise slits along the potato, spacing them ⅛ inch apart, being careful to not cut the potato completely through (the spoon handles will prevent you from cutting all the way through). Repeat with the remaining potatoes.
3. Rub the potatoes with the oil and season with salt.
4. In a small bowl, mix the butter, garlic, and parsley until smooth.
5. To cook the steak and potatoes: Install a crisper plate in each of the two baskets. Place the steaks in the Zone 1 basket and insert the basket in the unit. Place the potatoes in the Zone 2 basket and insert the basket in the unit.
6. Select Zone 1, select AIR FRY, set the temperature to 375°F, and set the time to 20 minutes.
7. Select Zone 2, select BAKE, set the temperature to 375°F, and set the time to 30 minutes. Select SMART FINISH.
8. Press START/PAUSE to begin cooking.
9. When both timers read 6 minutes, press START/PAUSE. Remove the Zone 1 basket and use silicone-tipped tongs to flip the steaks. Reinsert the basket in the unit. Remove the Zone 2 basket and spread the herb butter into the potatoes, being sure to work the butter in between the slices. Reinsert the basket and press START/PAUSE to resume cooking.
10. When cooking is complete, the steak should be cooked to your liking and the potato soft when pierced with a fork.
11. Remove the steaks from the basket and let rest for 5 minutes before slicing.

Cheeseburgers with Barbecue Potato Chips

Prep time: 15 minutes, plus 30 minutes to soak | Cook time: 15 minutes | Serves 4

- For the cheeseburgers
- 1 pound ground beef (85 percent lean)
- ¼ teaspoon kosher salt
- ¼ teaspoon freshly ground black pepper
- ½ teaspoon olive oil
- 4 slices American cheese
- 4 hamburger rolls
- For the potato chips
- 2 large russet potatoes
- 2 teaspoons vegetable oil
- 1½ teaspoons smoked paprika
- 1 teaspoon light brown sugar
- ½ teaspoon garlic powder
- ½ teaspoon kosher salt
- ¼ teaspoon chili powder

1. To prep the cheeseburgers: Season the beef with the salt and black pepper. Form the beef into 4 patties about 1 inch thick. Brush both sides of the beef patties with the oil.
2. To prep the potato chips: Fill a large bowl with ice water. Using a mandoline or sharp knife, cut the potatoes into very thin (⅛- to 1/16-inch) slices. Soak the potatoes in the ice water for 30 minutes.
3. Drain the potatoes and pat dry with a paper towel. Place in a large bowl and toss with the oil, smoked paprika, brown sugar, garlic powder, salt, and chili powder.
4. To cook the cheeseburgers and potato chips: Install a crisper plate in each of the two baskets. Place the burgers in the Zone 1 basket and insert the basket in the unit. Place the potato slices in the Zone 2 basket and insert the basket in the unit.
5. Select Zone 1, select AIR FRY, set the temperature to 390°F, and set the time to 12 minutes.
6. Select Zone 2, select AIR FRY, set the temperature to 390°F, and set the time to 15 minutes. Select SMART FINISH.
7. Press START/PAUSE to begin cooking.
8. At 5-minute intervals, press START/PAUSE. Remove the Zone 2 basket and shake the potato chips to keep them from sticking to each other. Reinsert the basket and press START/PAUSE to resume cooking.
9. When cooking is complete, the burgers should be cooked to your preferred doneness and the potato chips should be crisp and golden brown.
10. Top each burger patty in the basket with a slice of cheese. Turn the air fryer off and let the cheese melt inside the unit, or cover the basket with aluminum foil and let stand for 1 to 2 minutes, until the cheese is melted. Serve the cheeseburgers on buns with the chips on the side.

Beef and Bean Taquitos with Mexican Rice

Prep time: 15 minutes | Cook time: 15 minutes | Serves 4

- For the taquitos
- ½ pound ground beef (85 percent lean)
- 1 tablespoon taco seasoning
- 8 (6-inch) soft white corn tortillas
- Nonstick cooking spray
- ¾ cup canned refried beans
- ½ cup shredded Mexican blend cheese (optional)
- For the Mexican rice
- 1 cup dried instant white rice (not microwavable)
- 1½ cups chicken broth
- ¼ cup jarred salsa
- 2 tablespoons canned tomato sauce
- 1 tablespoon vegetable oil
- ½ teaspoon kosher salt

1. To prep the taquitos: In a large bowl, mix the ground beef and taco seasoning until well combined.
2. Mist both sides of each tortilla lightly with cooking spray.
3. To prep the Mexican rice: In the Zone 2 basket, combine the rice, broth, salsa, tomato sauce, oil, and salt. Stir well to ensure all of the rice is submerged in the liquid.
4. To cook the taquitos and rice: Install a crisper plate in the Zone 1 basket. Place the seasoned beef in the basket and insert the basket in the unit. Insert the Zone 2 basket in the unit.
5. Select Zone 1, select AIR FRY, set the temperature to 390°F, and set the time to 15 minutes.
6. Select Zone 2, select BAKE, set the temperature to 350°F, and set the time to 10 minutes. Select SMART FINISH.
7. Press START/PAUSE to begin cooking.
8. When the Zone 1 timer reads 10 minutes, press START/PAUSE. Remove the basket and transfer the beef to a medium bowl. Add the refried beans and cheese (if using) and combine well. Spoon 2 tablespoons of the filling onto each tortilla and roll tightly. Place the taquitos in the Zone 1 basket seam-side down. Reinsert the basket in the unit and press START/PAUSE to resume cooking.
9. When cooking is complete, the taquitos should be crisp and golden brown and the rice cooked through. Serve hot.

Garlic and Bacon Platter

Prep time: 10 minutes | Cook time: 30 minutes | Serves 4

- 4 potatoes, halved and peeled
- 6 garlic cloves, unpeeled and squashed
- 4 streaky cut rashers bacon
- 2 sprigs rosemary
- 1 tablespoon olive oil

1. Preheat your Air Fryer to 390-degree F
2. Add bacon, potatoes, rosemary, and garlic
3. Add oil and mix it well
4. Transfer the mix to a frying basket
5. Roast for 25-30 minutes
6. Serve and enjoy!

Pork Chops and Potatoes

Prep time: 15 minutes | Cook time:12 minutes| Serves 3

- 455g red potatoes
- Olive oil
- Salt and pepper
- 1 teaspoon garlic powder
- 1 teaspoon fresh rosemary, chopped
- 2 tablespoons brown sugar
- 1 tablespoon soy sauce
- 1 tablespoon Worcestershire sauce
- 1 teaspoon lemon juice
- 3 small pork chops

1. Mix potatoes and pork chops with remaining ingredients in a bowl.
2. Divide the ingredients in the air fryer baskets.
3. Return the air fryer basket 1 to Zone 1, and basket 2 to Zone 2 of the Ninja Foodi 2-Basket Air Fryer.
4. Choose the "Air Fry" mode for Zone 1 at 400 degrees F and 12 minutes of cooking time.
5. Select the "MATCH COOK" option to copy the settings for Zone 2.
6. Initiate cooking by pressing the START/PAUSE BUTTON.
7. Flip the chops and toss potatoes once cooked halfway through.
8. Serve warm.

Barbecue Pork Chop

Prep time: 5 minutes | Cook time: 10 minutes | Serves 4

- 4 pork chops
- ½ teaspoon dried paprika
- ½ teaspoon chili powder
- 1 teaspoon garlic powder
- 1 tablespoon brown sugar
- 1 teaspoon ground cumin
- ½ teaspoon all spice
- ½ teaspoon dry mustard
- Salt and pepper to taste

1. Combine rub ingredients in a bowl.
2. Coat both sides of pork chops with this mixture.
3. Add pork chops to the air fryer basket.
4. Select air fry setting.
5. Cook at 400 degrees F for 5 minutes per side.

Mongolian Beef with Sweet Chili Brussels Sprouts

Prep time: 10 minutes | Cook time: 20 minutes | Serves 4

- For the Mongolian beef
- 1 pound flank steak, cut into thin strips
- 1 tablespoon olive oil
- 2 tablespoons cornstarch
- ½ cup reduced-sodium soy sauce
- ½ cup packed light brown sugar
- 1 tablespoon chili paste (optional)
- 1 tablespoon minced garlic
- 1 tablespoon minced fresh ginger
- 2 scallions, chopped
- For the brussels sprouts
- 1 pound Brussels sprouts, halved lengthwise
- 1 tablespoon olive oil
- ½ cup gochujang sauce
- 2 tablespoons rice vinegar
- 1 tablespoon reduced-sodium soy sauce
- 1 tablespoon light brown sugar
- 1 teaspoon fresh garlic

1. To prep the Mongolian beef: In a large bowl, combine the flank steak and olive oil and toss to coat. Add the cornstarch and toss to coat.
2. In a small bowl, whisk together the soy sauce, brown sugar, chili paste (if using), garlic, and ginger. Set the soy sauce mixture aside.
3. To prep the Brussels sprouts: In a large bowl, combine the Brussels sprouts and oil and toss to coat.
4. In a small bowl, whisk together the gochujang sauce, vinegar, soy sauce, brown sugar, and garlic. Set the chili sauce mixture aside.
5. To cook the beef and Brussels sprouts: Install a crisper plate in each of the two baskets. Place the beef in the Zone 1 basket and insert the basket in the unit. Place the Brussels sprouts in the Zone 2 basket and insert the basket in the unit.
6. Select Zone 1, select AIR FRY, set the temperature to 390°F, and set the time to 15 minutes.
7. Select Zone 2, select AIR FRY, set the temperature to 400°F, and set the time to 20 minutes. Select SMART FINISH.
8. Press START/PAUSE to begin cooking.
9. When both timers read 5 minutes, press START/PAUSE. Remove the Zone 1 basket, add the reserved soy sauce mixture and the scallions, and toss with the beef. Reinsert the basket. Remove the Zone 2 basket, add the reserved chili sauce mixture, and toss with the Brussels sprouts. Reinsert the basket and press START/PAUSE to resume cooking.
10. When cooking is complete, the steak should be cooked through and the Brussels sprouts tender and slightly caramelized. Serve warm.

Beef Schnitzel

Prep time: 10 minutes | Cook time: 12 minutes | Serves 3

- 1 thin beef schnitzel
- 1 egg, whisked
- 2 tablespoons vegetable oil
- 2-ounce breadcrumbs
- 1 whole lemon

1. Preheat your Air Fryer to 356-degree F
2. Add breadcrumbs and vegetable oil into a bowl
3. Mix them well
4. Continue to stir the mixture
5. Dip the schnitzel into the Egg
6. Dredge the coated schnitzel into the bread crumb and coat well
7. Transfer them into Air fryer cooking basket
8. Cook for 12 minutes
9. Serve with lemon
10. Serve and enjoy!

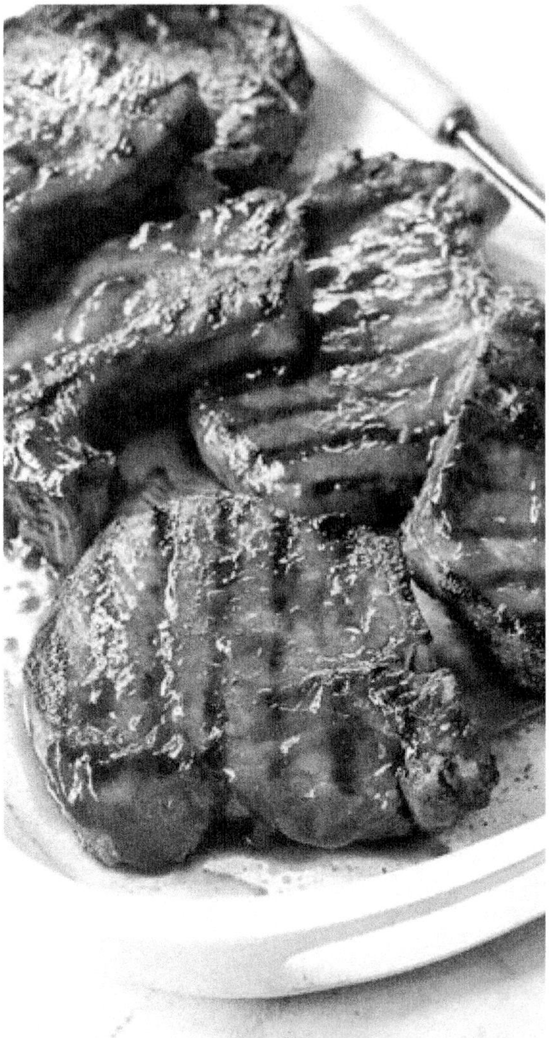

Italian Sausage Bites

Prep time: 5 minutes | Cook time: 10 minutes | Serves 4

- 1 lb. Italian sausage, sliced into smaller pieces
- 2 tablespoons olive oil
- Italian seasoning

1. Coat sausages with oil and seasoning.
2. Add sausages to the air fryer basket.
3. Spray with oil.
4. Cook at 400 degrees F for 5 minutes per side.

Roast Beef with Yorkshire Pudding

Prep time: 10 minutes, plus 15 minutes to rest | Cook time: 40 Minutes | Serves 6

- For the roast beef
- 3-pound beef roast, trimmed
- 1 tablespoon vegetable oil
- ½ teaspoon kosher salt
- ½ teaspoon freshly ground black pepper
- ½ teaspoon garlic powder
- ½ teaspoon onion powder
- ½ teaspoon dried thyme
- For the Yorkshire pudding
- 3 large eggs
- ¾ cup whole milk
- 2 tablespoons beef broth
- ¾ cup all-purpose flour
- ½ teaspoon kosher salt
- 2 teaspoons unsalted butter

1. To prep the roast beef: If necessary, trim the beef roast to fit in the Zone 1 basket. Rub the beef with the oil.
2. In a small bowl, combine the salt, black pepper, garlic powder, onion powder, and thyme. Rub the spice mixture all over the beef roast.
3. To prep the Yorkshire pudding: In a large bowl, whisk the eggs, milk, and beef broth until well combined. Whisk in the flour and salt to form a thin batter.
4. To cook the beef and Yorkshire pudding: Install a crisper plate in the Zone 1 basket. Place the beef roast in the basket and insert the basket in the unit. Place the butter in the Zone 2 basket and insert the basket in the unit.
5. Select Zone 1, select AIR FRY, set the temperature to 375°F, and set the time to 40 minutes for a medium-rare roast (set to 50 minutes for medium or 60 minutes for well done).
6. Select Zone 2, select BAKE, set the temperature to 400°F, and set the time to 20 minutes. Select SMART FINISH.
7. Press START/PAUSE to begin cooking.
8. When the Zone 2 timer reads 18 minutes, press START/PAUSE. Remove the basket and pour the batter into it. Reinsert the basket and press START/PAUSE to resume cooking.
9. When cooking is complete, the beef should be cooked to your liking and the Yorkshire pudding should be fluffy on the edges and set in the center.
10. Remove the beef from the basket and let rest for at least 15 minutes before slicing.
11. Cut the Yorkshire pudding into 6 servings and serve the sliced beef on top.

Italian Sausages with Peppers, Potatoes, and Onions

Prep time: 5 Minutes | Cook time: 22 Minutes | Serves 4

- For the peppers, potatoes, and onions
- 2 Yukon Gold potatoes, cut into ¼-inch slices
- 1 red bell pepper, sliced
- 1 yellow onion, sliced
- ¼ cup canned tomato sauce
- 1 tablespoon olive oil
- 1 teaspoon minced garlic
- ½ teaspoon dried oregano
- ¼ teaspoon kosher salt
- For the sausages
- 4 links Italian sausage

1. To prep the peppers, potatoes, and onions: In a large bowl, combine the potatoes, pepper, onion, tomato sauce, oil, garlic, oregano, and salt. Mix to combine.
2. To cook the sausage and vegetables: Install a crisper plate in each of the two baskets. Place the sausages in the Zone 1 basket and insert the basket in the unit. Place the potato mixture in the Zone 2 basket and insert the basket in the unit.
3. Select Zone 1, select AIR FRY, set the temperature to 390°F, and set the time to 22 minutes.
4. Select Zone 2, select ROAST, set the temperature to 375°F, and set the time to 20 minutes. Select SMART FINISH.
5. Press START/PAUSE to begin cooking.
6. When cooking is complete, the sausages will be cooked through and the vegetables tender.
7. Slice the sausages into rounds, then mix them into the potato and pepper mixture. Serve.

Steak and Asparagus Bundles

Prep time: 15 minutes | Cook time: 10 minutes| Serves 6

- 907g flank steak, cut into 6 pieces
- Salt and black pepper, to taste
- ½ cup tamari sauce
- 2 cloves garlic, crushed
- 455g asparagus, trimmed
- 3 capsicums, sliced
- ¼ cup balsamic vinegar
- 79 ml beef broth
- 2 tablespoons unsalted butter
- Olive oil spray

1. Mix steaks with black pepper, tamari sauce, and garlic in a Ziplock bag.
2. Seal the bag, shake well and refrigerate for 1 hour.
3. Place the steaks on the working surface and top each with asparagus and capsicums.
4. Roll the steaks and secure them with toothpicks.
5. Place these rolls in the air fryer baskets.
6. Return the air fryer basket 1 to Zone 1, and basket 2 to Zone 2 of the Ninja Foodi 2-Basket Air Fryer.
7. Choose the "Air Fry" mode for Zone 1 and set the temperature to 400 degrees F and 10 minutes of cooking time.
8. Select the "MATCH COOK" option to copy the settings for Zone 2.
9. Initiate cooking by pressing the START/PAUSE BUTTON.
10. Meanwhile, cook broth with butter and vinegar in a saucepan.
11. Cook this mixture until reduced by half and adjust seasoning with black pepper and salt.
12. Serve the steak rolls with the prepared sauce.

Marinated Steak & Mushrooms

Prep time: 15 minutes | Cook time: 10 minutes| Serves 4

- 450g rib-eye steak, cut into ½-inch pieces
- 2 tsp dark soy sauce
- 2 tsp light soy sauce
- 15ml lime juice
- 15ml rice wine
- 15ml oyster sauce
- 1 tbsp garlic, chopped
- 8 mushrooms, sliced
- 2 tbsp ginger, grated
- 1 tsp cornstarch
- ¼ tsp pepper

1. Add steak pieces, mushrooms, and the remaining ingredients to a zip-lock bag. Seal the bag and place it in the refrigerator for 2 hours.
2. Insert a crisper plate in the Ninja Foodi air fryer baskets.
3. Remove the steak pieces and mushrooms from the marinade and place them in both baskets.
4. Select zone 1, then select "air fry" mode and set the temperature to 380 degrees F for 10 minutes. Press "match" to match zone 2 settings to zone 1. Press "start/stop" to begin. Stir halfway through.

Beef and Tomato Balls

Prep time: 10 minutes | Cook time: 5 minutes | Serves 4

- ¾ pounds ground beef
- 3 tablespoons almond meal
- 1 tablespoon fresh parsley, chopped
- 1 whole egg
- ½ tablespoon fresh thyme leaves, chopped
- 1 small onion, chopped
- Salt and pepper to taste

1. Preheat your Air Fryer to 390-degree F
2. Chop onion and keep them aside
3. Add all the listed ingredients into a bowl
4. Mix them well
5. Make 12 balls
6. Transfer balls to the Fryer
7. Cook for 8 minutes and transfer the balls to the oven
8. Add tomatoes sauce and drown the balls
9. Transfer the dish to your Air Fryer
10. Cook for 5 minutes at 300 degrees F
11. Stir occasionally
12. Serve and enjoy!

Roast Souvlaki-Style Pork with Lemon-Feta Baby Potatoes

Prep time: 10 Minutes | Cook time: 40 Minutes | Serves 4

- For the pork
- 1½ pounds pork tenderloin, cut into bite-size cubes
- ¼ cup olive oil
- ¼ cup fresh lemon juice
- 2 teaspoons minced garlic
- 2 teaspoons honey
- 1½ teaspoons dried oregano
- ¼ teaspoon kosher salt
- ¼ teaspoon freshly ground black pepper
- For the potatoes
- 1 pound baby red or yellow potatoes, halved
- 1 tablespoon olive oil
- Grated zest and juice of 1 lemon
- ½ teaspoon kosher salt
- ¼ teaspoon freshly ground black pepper
- ⅓ cup crumbled feta cheese
- 2 tablespoons chopped fresh parsley

1. To prep the pork: In a large bowl, combine the pork, oil, lemon juice, garlic, honey, oregano, salt, and black pepper. If desired, cover and refrigerate up to 24 hours.
2. To prep the potatoes: In a large bowl, combine the potatoes, oil, lemon zest, lemon juice, salt, and black pepper. Mix to coat the potatoes.
3. To cook the pork and potatoes: Install a crisper plate in each of the two baskets. Place the pork in the Zone 1 basket and insert the basket in the unit. Place the potatoes in the Zone 2 basket and insert the basket in the unit.
4. Select Zone 1, select ROAST, set the temperature to 390°F, and set the time to 20 minutes.
5. Select Zone 2, select AIR FRY, set the temperature to 400°F, and set the time to 40 minutes. Select SMART FINISH.
6. Press START/PAUSE to begin cooking.
7. When cooking is complete, the pork will be cooked through (an instant-read thermometer should read 145°F) and the potatoes will be tender and beginning to brown around the edges.
8. Stir the feta and parsley into the potatoes. Serve the pork and potatoes while hot.

Garlic-Rosemary Pork Loin with Scalloped Potatoes and Cauliflower

Prep time: 15 minutes, plus 15 minutes to rest | Cook time: 50 Minutes | Serves 6

- For the pork loin
- 2 pounds pork loin roast
- 2 tablespoons vegetable oil
- 2 teaspoons dried thyme
- 2 teaspoons dried crushed rosemary
- 1 teaspoon minced garlic
- ¾ teaspoon kosher salt
- For the scalloped potatoes and cauliflower
- 1 teaspoon vegetable oil
- ¾ pound Yukon Gold potatoes, peeled and very thinly sliced
- 1½ cups cauliflower florets
- ¼ teaspoon kosher salt
- ¼ teaspoon freshly ground black pepper
- 1 tablespoon very cold unsalted butter, grated
- 3 tablespoons all-purpose flour
- 1 cup whole milk
- 1 cup shredded Gruyère cheese

1. To prep the pork loin: Coat the pork with the oil. Season with thyme, rosemary, garlic, and salt.
2. To prep the potatoes and cauliflower: Brush the bottom and sides of the Zone 2 basket with the oil. Add one-third of the potatoes to the bottom of the basket and arrange in a single layer. Top with ½ cup of cauliflower florets. Sprinkle a third of the salt and black pepper on top. Scatter one-third of the butter on top and sprinkle on 1 tablespoon of flour. Repeat this step twice more for a total of three layers.
3. Pour the milk over the layered potatoes and cauliflower; it should just cover the top layer. Top with the Gruyère.
4. To cook the pork and scalloped vegetables: Install a crisper plate in the Zone 1 basket. Place the pork loin in the basket and insert the basket in the unit. Insert the Zone 2 basket in the unit.
5. Select Zone 1, select AIR FRY, set the temperature to 390°F, and set the time to 50 minutes.
6. Select Zone 2, select BAKE, set the temperature to 350°F, and set the time to 45 minutes. Select SMART FINISH.
7. Press START/PAUSE to begin cooking.
8. When cooking is complete, the pork will be cooked through (an instant-read thermometer should read 145°F) and the potatoes and cauliflower will be tender.
9. Let the pork rest for at least 15 minutes before slicing and serving with the scalloped vegetables.

Pigs in a Blanket with Spinach-Artichoke Stuffed Mushrooms

Prep time: 10 minutes | Cook time: 15 minutes | Serves 4

- For the pigs in a blanket
- Half an 8-ounce tube refrigerated crescent roll dough
- 4 hot dogs
- ½ teaspoon everything bagel seasoning (optional)
- For the stuffed mushrooms
- 1 cup frozen chopped spinach, thawed and drained
- 1 (14-ounce) can artichoke hearts, drained and chopped
- 2 ounces (¼ cup) cream cheese, at room temperature
- ¼ cup grated Parmesan cheese
- ½ teaspoon garlic powder
- 1 (8-ounce) package whole cremini mushrooms, stems removed

1. To prep the pigs in a blanket: Unroll the crescent roll dough. It will be scored into 4 triangular pieces, but leave them in place and pinch together at the seams to form 1 large square of dough. Cut the dough into 4 strips.
2. Wrap one strip of dough around each hot dog, starting with a short end of the strips and wrapping in a spiral motion around the hot dog. If desired, sprinkle each pig in a blanket with everything bagel seasoning.
3. To prep the stuffed mushrooms: In a medium bowl, combine the spinach, artichoke hearts, cream cheese, Parmesan, and garlic powder. Stuff about 1 tablespoon of filling into each mushroom cap.
4. To cook the pigs in a blanket and mushrooms: Install a crisper plate in each of the two baskets. Place the pigs in a blanket in the Zone 1 basket and insert the basket in the unit. Place the mushrooms in the Zone 2 basket and insert the basket in the unit.
5. Select Zone 1, select AIR FRY, set the temperature to 370°F, and set the time to 8 minutes.
6. Select Zone 2, select BAKE, set the temperature to 370°F, and set the time to 15 minutes. Select SMART FINISH.
7. Press START/PAUSE to begin cooking.
8. When cooking is complete, the crescent roll dough should be cooked through and golden brown, and the mushrooms should be tender.

Pork Tenderloin with Brown Sugar-Pecan Sweet Potatoes

Prep time: 5 minutes, plus 5 minutes to rest | Cook time: 45 Minutes | Serves 4

- For the pork tenderloin
- 1½ pounds pork tenderloin
- 2 teaspoons vegetable oil
- ½ teaspoon kosher salt
- ½ teaspoon poultry seasoning
- For the sweet potatoes
- 4 teaspoons unsalted butter, at room temperature
- 2 tablespoons dark brown sugar
- ¼ cup chopped pecans
- 4 small sweet potatoes

1. To prep the pork: Coat the pork tenderloin with the oil, then rub with the salt and poultry seasoning.
2. To prep the sweet potatoes: In a small bowl, mix the butter, brown sugar, and pecans until well combined.
3. To cook the pork and sweet potatoes: Install a crisper plate in the Zone 1 basket. Place the pork tenderloin in the basket and insert the basket in the unit. Place the sweet potatoes in the Zone 2 basket and insert the basket in the unit.
4. Select Zone 1, select AIR FRY, set the temperature to 390°F, and set the time to 25 minutes.
5. Select Zone 2, select BAKE, set the temperature to 400°F, and set the time to 45 minutes. Select SMART FINISH.
6. Press START/PAUSE to begin cooking.
7. When the Zone 2 timer reads 10 minutes, press START/PAUSE. Remove the basket. Slice the sweet potatoes open lengthwise. Divide the pecan mixture among the potatoes. Reinsert the basket and press START/PAUSE to resume cooking.
8. When cooking is complete, the pork will be cooked through (an instant-read thermometer should read 145°F) and the potatoes will be soft and their flesh fluffy.
9. Transfer the pork loin to a plate or cutting board and let rest for at least 5 minutes before slicing and serving.

Blackened Pork Chops

Prep time: 10 minutes | Cook time: 15 minutes | Serves 4

- 1 lb. pork loin
- 1 teaspoon paprika
- 1 teaspoon dried thyme
- 1 teaspoon chili powder
- 1 teaspoon cayenne pepper
- 1 teaspoon garlic powder
- 1 teaspoon sugar
- Salt and pepper to taste

1. Mix all the spices in a bowl.
2. Cover both sides of pork with this mixture.
3. Add pork to the air fryer basket.
4. Set it to air fry.
5. Cook at 360 degrees F for 6 to 8 minutes per side.

Pork Katsu with Seasoned Rice

Prep time: 15 minutes | Cook time: 15 minutes | Serves 4

- For the pork katsu
- 4 thin-sliced boneless pork chops (4 ounces each)
- 2 tablespoons all-purpose flour
- 2 large eggs
- 1 cup panko bread crumbs
- ¼ teaspoon kosher salt
- ¼ teaspoon freshly ground black pepper
- 1 teaspoon vegetable oil
- 3 tablespoons ketchup
- 3 tablespoons Worcestershire sauce
- 1 tablespoon oyster sauce
- ⅛ teaspoon granulated sugar
- For the rice
- 2 cups dried instant rice (not microwavable)
- 2½ cups water
- 1 tablespoon sesame oil
- 1 teaspoon soy sauce
- 1 tablespoon toasted sesame seeds
- 3 scallions, sliced

1. To prep the pork katsu: Place the pork chops between two slices of plastic wrap. Using a meat mallet or rolling pin, pound the pork into ½-inch-thick cutlets.
2. Set up a breading station with three small shallow bowls. Place the flour in the first bowl. In the second bowl, whisk the eggs. Combine the panko, salt, and black pepper in the third bowl.
3. Bread the cutlets in this order: First, dip them in the flour, coating both sides. Then, dip them into the beaten egg. Finally, coat them in panko, gently pressing the bread crumbs to adhere to the pork. Drizzle both sides of the cutlets with the oil.
4. To prep the rice: In the Zone 2 basket, combine the rice, water, sesame oil, and soy sauce. Stir well to ensure all of the rice is submerged in the liquid.
5. To cook the pork and rice: Install a crisper plate in the Zone 1 basket. Place the pork in the basket and insert the basket in the unit. Insert the Zone 2 basket in the unit.
6. Select Zone 1, select AIR FRY, set the temperature to 390°F, and set the time to 15 minutes.
7. Select Zone 2, select BAKE, set the temperature to 350°F, and set the time to 10 minutes. Select SMART FINISH.
8. Press START/PAUSE to begin cooking.
9. When the Zone 1 timer reads 10 minutes, press START/PAUSE. Remove the basket and use silicone-tipped tongs to flip the pork. Reinsert the basket and press START/PAUSE to resume cooking.
10. When cooking is complete, the pork should be crisp and cooked through and the rice tender.
11. Stir the sesame seeds and scallions into the rice. For the sauce to go with the pork, in a small bowl, whisk together the ketchup, Worcestershire sauce, oyster sauce, and sugar. Drizzle the sauce over the pork and serve with the hot rice.

Barbecue Ribs with Roasted Green Beans and Shallots

Prep time: 5 Minutes | Cook time: 40 Minutes | Serves 4

- For the ribs
- 1 tablespoon light brown sugar
- 1 tablespoon smoked paprika
- 1 tablespoon chili powder
- 2 teaspoons kosher salt
- 1 teaspoon freshly ground black pepper
- 1 teaspoon garlic powder
- ¼ teaspoon cayenne pepper (optional)
- 2 pounds pork ribs
- 1 cup barbecue sauce (your favorite), for serving
- For the green beans and shallots
- 1 pound green beans, trimmed
- 2 shallots, sliced
- 1 tablespoon olive oil
- ¼ teaspoon kosher salt

1. To prep the ribs: In a small bowl, combine the brown sugar, paprika, chili powder, salt, black pepper, garlic powder, and cayenne (if using).
2. Rub the spice blend all over both sides of the ribs.
3. To prep the green beans and shallots: In a large bowl, combine the green beans, shallots, and oil. Toss to coat. Season with the salt.
4. To cook the ribs and vegetables: Install a crisper plate in each of the two baskets. Place the ribs in the Zone 1 basket and insert the basket in the unit. Place the green beans in the Zone 2 basket and insert the basket in the unit.
5. Select Zone 1, select AIR FRY, set the temperature to 375°F, and set the time to 40 minutes.
6. Select Zone 2, select ROAST, set the temperature to 400°F, and set the time to 20 minutes. Select SMART FINISH.
7. Press START/PAUSE to begin cooking.
8. When the Zone 1 timer reads 10 minutes, press START/PAUSE. Increase the temperature of Zone 1 to 400°F. Press START/PAUSE to resume cooking.
9. When cooking is complete, an instant-read thermometer inserted into the ribs should read 170°F and the green beans should be tender-crisp. Serve topped with your favorite barbecue sauce.

Curry-Crusted Lamb Chops with Baked Brown Sugar Acorn Squash

Prep time: 10 minutes, plus 5 minutes to rest | Cook time: 20 Minutes | Serves 4

- For the lamb chops
- 4 lamb loin chops (4 ounces each)
- 1 tablespoon olive oil
- 2 teaspoons curry powder
- ¼ teaspoon kosher salt
- For the acorn squash
- 2 small acorn squash
- 4 teaspoons dark brown sugar
- 2 teaspoons salted butter
- ⅛ teaspoon kosher salt

1. To prep the lamb chops: Brush both sides of the lamb chops with the oil and season with the curry powder and salt.
2. To prep the acorn squash: Cut the squash in half through the stem end and remove the seeds. Place 1 teaspoon of brown sugar and ½ teaspoon of butter into the well of each squash half.
3. To cook the lamb and squash: Install a crisper plate in each of the two baskets. Place the lamb chops in the Zone 1 basket and insert the basket in the unit. Place the squash cut-side up in the Zone 2 basket and insert the basket in the unit.
4. Select Zone 1, select AIR FRY, set the temperature to 400°F, and set the timer to 15 minutes.
5. Select Zone 2, select BAKE, set the temperature to 400°F, and set the time to 20 minutes. Select SMART FINISH.
6. Press START/PAUSE to begin cooking.
7. When both timers read 5 minutes, press START/PAUSE. Remove the Zone 1 basket and use a pair of silicone-tipped tongs to flip the lamb chops. Reinsert the basket in the unit. Remove the Zone 2 basket and spoon the melted butter and sugar over the top edges of the squash. Reinsert the basket and press START/PAUSE to resume cooking.
8. When cooking is complete, the lamb should be cooked to your liking and the squash soft when pierced with a fork.
9. Remove the lamb chops from the basket and let rest for 5 minutes. Season the acorn squash with salt before serving.

Chapter 6
Fish and Seafood Recipes

Tuna Steak

Prep time: 10 minutes | Cook time: 15 minutes | Serves 4

- 2 tablespoons olive oil
- 1 tablespoon lemon zest
- 2 tablespoons lemon juice
- 2 teaspoon dried thyme
- 2 cloves garlic, minced
- Salt and pepper to taste
- 4 tuna steaks

1. In a bowl, combine all ingredients except tuna steaks.
2. Add tuna to the bowl.
3. Marinate in the mixture for 30 minutes.
4. Add tuna to the air fryer basket.
5. Cook at 380 degrees F for 5 to 7 minutes per side.

Coconut Crusted Tilapia

Prep time: 10 minutes | Cook time: 10 minutes | Serves 4

- ½ cup coconut flour
- 1 cup coconut flakes
- Salt to taste
- 3 eggs, beaten
- 4 tilapia fillets

1. Mix flour, coconut flakes and salt in a bowl.
2. Add eggs to another bowl.
3. Dip fish in the eggs and then dredge with coconut mixture.
4. Add fish to the air fryer basket.
5. Set it to air fry.
6. Cook at 400 degrees F for 4 to 5 minutes per side.

Baked Salmon in Honey Lemon Sauce

Prep time: 10 minutes | Cook time: 30 minutes | Serves 2

- ½ cup butter, melted
- 4 tablespoons honey
- 3 tablespoons lemon juice
- Salt and pepper to taste
- 2 salmon fillets

1. Mix all the ingredients except fish in a bowl.
2. Brush both sides of fish with sauce.
3. Add to the air fryer basket.
4. Select bake setting.
5. Bake at 390 degrees F for 15 minutes per side.

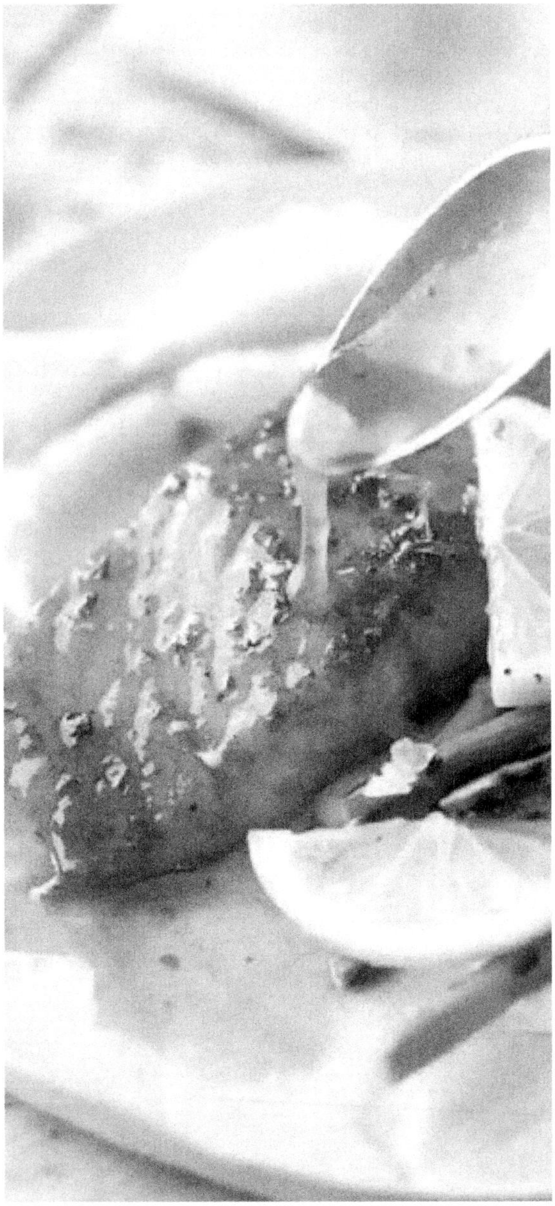

Salmon in Lemon Mustard Sauce

Prep time: 10 minutes | Cook time: 20 minutes | Serves: 2

- 2 tablespoons olive oil
- 2 cloves garlic, minced
- 2 tablespoons lemon juice
- 1 tablespoon mustard
- ½ teaspoon ground thyme
- Salt and pepper to taste
- 2 salmon fillets

1. Mix oil, garlic, lemon juice, mustard, thyme, salt and pepper in a bowl.
2. Brush both sides of salmon with this mixture.
3. Place salmon inside the air fryer basket.
4. Choose bake function.
5. Bake at 400 degrees F for 10 minutes per side.

Salmon Patties

Prep time: 10 minutes | Cook time: 10 minutes | Serves 4

- 15 oz. salmon flakes
- 1 egg, beaten
- ¼ cup onion, chopped
- ½ cup breadcrumbs
- 1 teaspoon dill weed
- Salt and pepper to taste

1. Mix all the ingredients in a bowl.
2. Shape mixture into 4 patties.
3. Place 2 patties in 1 air fryer basket and 2 patties in the other air fryer basket.
4. Select air fry setting.
5. Set temperature to 370 degrees F.
6. Cook for 5 minutes per side.

Honey Glazed Salmon

Prep time: 10 minutes | Cook time: 12 minutes | Serves 2

- 2 salmon fillets
- ¾ teaspoon toasted sesame oil
- 1 teaspoon sesame seeds
- ½ tablespoon low-sodium soy sauce
- ½ tablespoon honey
- ¼ teaspoon crushed chili flakes
- Salt and pepper, to taste

1. In a shallow dish, add soy sauce, salt, pepper and oil. Whisk well.
2. Pour the mixture over salmon-fillets and rub all over the fish.
3. Cover the dish and place the mixture in refrigerator for about 15 minutes.
4. Remove the salmon fillets from refrigerator and shake off the excess marinade.
5. Line each basket of "Zone 1" and "Zone 2" of Ninja Foodi 2-Basket Air Fryer with a piece of foil.
6. Press your chosen zone - "Zone 1" or "Zone 2" and then rotate the knob to select "Air Fry".
7. Set the heat to 180 degrees C and then set the time for 5 minutes to preheat.
8. After preheating, arrange salmon fillets into the basket of each zone.
9. Brush with honey and sprinkle with chili flakes and sesame seeds.
10. Slide the basket into the Air Fryer and set the time for 12 minutes.
11. After cooking time is completed, remove the salmon fillets from Air Fryer and serve hot.

Lemon & Herb Roasted Salmon

Prep time: 10 minutes | Cook time: 10 minutes | Serves: 2

- 2 tablespoons butter, melted
- 2 cloves garlic, minced
- 1 teaspoon Italian seasoning mix
- ½ teaspoon red pepper flakes
- Salt and pepper to taste
- 1 tablespoon lemon juice
- 1 teaspoon lemon zest
- 2 salmon fillets

1. Combine all the ingredients except salmon fillets in a bowl.
2. Coat salmon with the butter mixture.
3. Transfer to the air fryer basket.
4. Choose air fry setting.
5. Cook at 400 degrees F for 10 minutes per side.

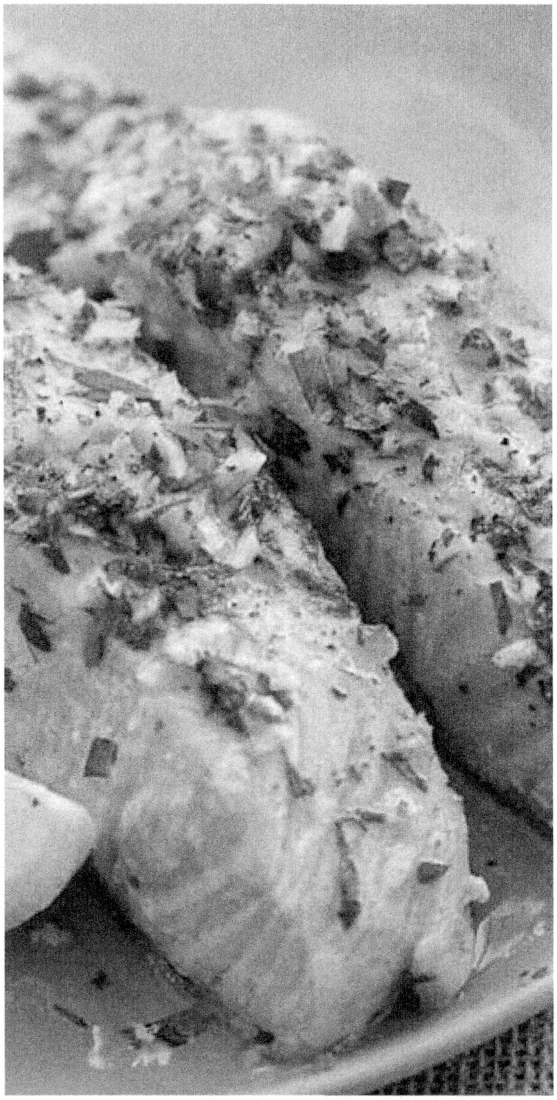

Swordfish Fillet with Mango Salsa

Prep time: 10 minutes | Cook time: 10 minutes | Serves 4

- 4 swordfish steaks
- Salt and pepper to taste
- Salsa
- 2 mangoes, sliced into cubes
- ½ cup red onion, chopped
- 1 jalapeno pepper, diced
- ½ cup cilantro, sliced
- 2 tablespoons lime juice

1. Sprinkle both sides of fish with salt and pepper.
2. Let sit for 5 minutes.
3. Add fish to the air fryer basket.
4. Select roast setting.
5. Cook at 400 degrees F for 5 minutes per side.
6. Mix salsa ingredients in a bowl.
7. Top fish with salsa and serve.

Cod with Creamy Garlic Pesto Sauce

Prep time: 10 minutes | Cook time: 15 minutes | Serves 4

- 4 cod fillets
- 1 tablespoon olive oil
- 2 cloves garlic, minced
- ¼ cup basil pesto
- 3 tablespoons cream
- Salt and pepper to taste

1. Add oil to a pan over medium heat.
2. Cook garlic for 30 seconds, stirring frequently.
3. Stir in the remaining ingredients except fish.
4. Simmer for 5 minutes. Set aside.
5. Season fish with salt and pepper.
6. Add fish to the air fryer basket.
7. Set it to air fry.
8. Cook at 350 degrees F for 5 minutes per side.
9. Pour sauce over the fish and serve.

Asparagus Salmon

Prep time: 10 minutes | Cook time: 13 minutes | Serves 4

- 3 tablespoons lemon juice
- 4 tablespoons fresh dill, roughly chopped
- 4 salmon fillets
- 2 tablespoons olive oil
- 4 tablespoons fresh parsley, roughly chopped
- 900g asparagus
- Salt and pepper, to taste

1. In a small dish, mix lemon juice, olive oil, salt, pepper, dill and parsley.
2. Add salmon fillets in the mixture, coat well and set aside.
3. Now, add asparagus in the dill mixture and mix well.
4. Grease basket of Ninja Foodi 2-Basket Air Fryer.
5. Press your chosen zone - "Zone 1" or "Zone 2" and then rotate the knob to select "Air Fry".
6. Set the heat to 200 degrees C and then set the time for 5 minutes to preheat.
7. After preheating, arrange asparagus into the basket of each zone.
8. Slide the basket into the Air Fryer and set the time for 13 minutes.
9. After 3 minutes of cooking, arrange 2 salmon fillets on top of asparagus in each basket.
10. After cooking time is completed, remove the salmon fillets and asparagus from Air Fryer and serve hot.

Beer-Battered Fish

Prep time: 30 minutes | Cook time: 12 minutes | Serves 2

- 2 cod fillets, sliced into strips
- Cooking spray
- Batter
- 1 cup all-purpose flour
- 1 teaspoon baking soda
- 2 tablespoons cornstarch
- 8 oz. beer
- 1 egg
- Salt and pepper to taste
- Flour mixture for dredging
- 1 cup all-purpose flour
- 1 teaspoon paprika
- 1 teaspoon garlic powder
- 1 teaspoon Old Bay seasoning

1. Combine the batter ingredients in a bowl.
2. In another bowl, mix the flour mixture ingredients.
3. Spray fish with oil.
4. Coat with batter and dredge with flour.
5. Add to the air fryer basket.
6. Select air fry setting.
7. Cook at 380 degrees F for 6 to 7 minutes per side.

Broiled Teriyaki Salmon with Eggplant in Stir-Fry Sauce

Prep time: 5 minutes | Cook time: 25 minutes | Serves 4

- For the teriyaki salmon
- 4 salmon fillets (6 ounces each)
- ½ cup teriyaki sauce
- 3 scallions, sliced
- For the eggplant
- ¼ cup reduced-sodium soy sauce
- ¼ cup packed light brown sugar
- 1 tablespoon minced fresh ginger
- 1 tablespoon minced garlic
- 2 teaspoons sesame oil
- ¼ teaspoon red pepper flakes
- 1 eggplant, peeled and cut into bite-size cubes
- Nonstick cooking spray

1. To prep the teriyaki salmon: Brush the top of each salmon fillet with the teriyaki sauce.
2. To prep the eggplant: In a small bowl, whisk together the soy sauce, brown sugar, ginger, garlic, sesame oil, and red pepper flakes. Set the stir-fry sauce aside.
3. Spritz the eggplant cubes with cooking spray.
4. To cook the salmon and eggplant: Install a crisper plate in each of the two baskets. Place the salmon in a single layer in the Zone 1 basket and insert the basket in the unit. Place the eggplant in the Zone 2 basket and insert the basket in the unit.
5. Select Zone 1, select AIR BROIL, set the temperature to 450°F, and set the time to 8 minutes.
6. Select Zone 2, select AIR FRY, set the temperature to 390°F, and set the time to 25 minutes. Select SMART FINISH.
7. Press START/PAUSE to begin cooking.
8. When the Zone 2 timer reads 5 minutes, press START/PAUSE. Remove the basket and pour the stir-fry sauce evenly over the eggplant. Shake or stir to coat the eggplant cubes in the sauce. Reinsert the basket and press START/PAUSE to resume cooking.
9. When cooking is complete, the salmon should be cooked to your liking and the eggplant tender and slightly caramelized. Serve hot.

Bang Bang Shrimp with Roasted Bok Choy

Prep time: 15 minutes | Cook time: 13 minutes | Serves 4

- For the bang bang shrimp
- ½ cup all-purpose flour
- 2 large eggs
- 1 cup panko bread crumbs
- 1 pound peeled shrimp (tails removed), thawed if frozen
- Nonstick cooking spray
- ½ cup mayonnaise
- ¼ cup Thai sweet chili sauce
- ¼ teaspoon sriracha
- For the bok choy
- 1 tablespoon reduced-sodium soy sauce
- 1 teaspoon minced garlic
- 1 teaspoon sesame oil
- 1 teaspoon minced fresh ginger
- 1½ pounds baby bok choy, halved lengthwise
- 1 tablespoon toasted sesame seeds

1. To prep the shrimp: Set up a breading station with three small shallow bowls. Place the flour in the first bowl. In the second bowl, whisk the eggs. Place the panko in the third bowl.
2. Bread the shrimp in this order: First, dip them into the flour, coating both sides. Then, dip into the beaten egg. Finally, coat them in the panko, gently pressing the bread crumbs to adhere to the shrimp. Spritz both sides of the shrimp with cooking spray.
3. To prep the bok choy: In a small bowl, whisk together the soy sauce, garlic, sesame oil, and ginger.
4. To cook the shrimp and bok choy: Install a crisper plate in the Zone 1 basket. Place the shrimp in the basket in a single layer and insert the basket in the unit. Place the boy choy cut-side up in the Zone 2 basket. Pour the sauce over the bok choy and insert the basket in the unit.
5. Select Zone 1, select AIR FRY, set the temperature to 390°F, and set the timer to 13 minutes.
6. Select Zone 2, select BAKE, set the temperature to 370°F, and set the timer to 8 minutes. Select SMART FINISH.
7. Press START/PAUSE to begin cooking.
8. When cooking is complete, the shrimp should be cooked through and golden brown and the bok choy soft and slightly caramelized.
9. In a large bowl, whisk together the mayonnaise, sweet chili sauce, and sriracha. Add the shrimp and toss to coat.
10. Sprinkle the bok choy with the sesame seeds and serve hot alongside the shrimp.

Crispy Haddock

Prep time: 10 minutes | Cook time: 12 minutes | Serves 4

- ½ cup all-purpose flour
- 6 tablespoons mayonnaise
- 2 eggs
- 3 cups breadcrumbs
- Salt and pepper to taste
- 4 haddock fish fillets

1. Add flour to a bowl.
2. Mix mayo and egg in another bowl.
3. In the third bowl, mix breadcrumbs, salt and pepper.
4. Coat fish with flour.
5. Dip in mayo mixture and dredge with breadcrumb mixture.
6. Place in the air fryer basket.
7. Set it to air fry.
8. Cook at 350 degrees F for 4 to 6 minutes per side.

Blackened Mahimahi with Honey-Roasted Carrots

Prep time: 5 minutes | Cook time: 30 minutes | Serves 4

- For the mahimahi
- 4 mahimahi fillets (4 ounces each)
- 1 tablespoon olive oil
- 1 tablespoon blackening seasoning
- Lemon wedges, for serving
- For the carrots
- 1 pound carrots, peeled and cut into ½-inch rounds
- 2 teaspoons vegetable oil
- ½ teaspoon kosher salt
- ¼ teaspoon freshly ground black pepper
- 1 tablespoon salted butter, cut into small pieces
- 1 tablespoon honey
- 2 tablespoons chopped fresh parsley

1. To prep the mahimahi: Brush both sides of the fish with the oil and sprinkle with the blackening seasoning.
2. To prep the carrots: In a large bowl, combine the carrots, oil, salt, and black pepper. Stir well to coat the carrots with the oil.
3. To cook the mahimahi and carrots: Install a crisper plate in each of the two baskets. Place the fish in the Zone 1 basket and insert the basket in the unit. Place the carrots in the Zone 2 basket and insert the basket in the unit.
4. Select Zone 1, select AIR FRY, set the temperature to 380°F, and set the timer to 14 minutes.
5. Select Zone 2, select ROAST, set the temperature to 400°F, and set the timer to 30 minutes. Select SMART FINISH.
6. Press START/PAUSE to begin cooking.
7. When the Zone 2 timer reads 15 minutes, press START/PAUSE. Remove the basket and scatter the butter over the carrots, then drizzle them with the honey. Reinsert the basket and press START/PAUSE to resume cooking.
8. When cooking is complete, the fish should be cooked through and the carrots soft.
9. Stir the parsley into the carrots. Serve the fish with lemon wedges.

Teriyaki Salmon

Prep time: 10 minutes | Cook time: 15 minutes | Serves 3

- 8 tsp Less Sodium Teriyaki
- 3 tsp honey
- 2 cubes of frozen garlic
- 2 tsp extra virgin olive oil
- 3 pieces of wild salmon

1. Whisk everything together to make the marinade.
2. Pour over defrosted fish and marinate for 20 minutes.
3. Press your chosen zone - "Zone 1" or "Zone 2" and then rotate the knob to select "Air Fry".
4. Set the temperature to 175 degrees C, and then set the time for 5 minutes to preheat.
5. After preheating, place a foil sheet on each basket, spray the Air-Fryer basket of each zone with cooking spray, arrange them in a single layer, and spritz them with cooking spray.
6. Slide the basket into the Air Fryer and set the time for 12 minutes.
7. Carefully turn them and cook them 6 minutes longer.
8. After cooking time is completed, place them on a serving plate and serve.

Tilapia with Mojo and Crispy Plantains

Prep time: 10 minutes, plus 15 minutes to soak | Cook time: 30 minutes | Serves 4

- For the tilapia
- 4 tilapia fillets (6 ounces each)
- 2 tablespoons all-purpose flour
- Nonstick cooking spray
- ¼ cup freshly squeezed orange juice
- 3 tablespoons fresh lime juice
- 2 tablespoons olive oil
- 1 tablespoon minced garlic
- ½ teaspoon ground cumin
- ¼ teaspoon kosher salt
- For the plantains
- 1 large green plantain
- 2 cups cold water
- 2 teaspoons kosher salt
- Nonstick cooking spray

1. To prep the tilapia: Dust both sides of the tilapia fillets with the flour, then spritz with cooking spray.
2. In a small bowl, whisk together the orange juice, lime juice, oil, garlic, cumin, and salt. Set the mojo sauce aside.
3. To prep the plantains: Cut the ends from the plantain, then remove and discard the peel. Slice the plantain into 1-inch rounds.
4. In a large bowl, combine the water, salt, and plantains. Let soak for 15 minutes.
5. Drain the plantains and pat them dry with paper towels. Spray with cooking spray.
6. To cook the tilapia and plantains: Install a crisper plate in each of the two baskets. Place the tilapia in a single layer in the Zone 1 basket (work in batches if needed) and insert the basket in the unit. Place the plantains in the Zone 2 basket and insert the basket in the unit.
7. Select Zone 1, select AIR FRY, set the temperature to 390°F, and set the timer to 10 minutes.
8. Select Zone 2, select AIR FRY, set the temperature to 390°F, and set the timer to 30 minutes. Select SMART FINISH.
9. Press START/PAUSE to begin cooking.
10. When the Zone 2 timer reads 10 minutes, press START/PAUSE. Remove the basket and use silicone-tipped tongs to transfer the plantains, which should be tender, to a cutting board. Use the bottom of a heavy glass to smash each plantain flat. Spray both sides with cooking spray and place them back in the basket. Reinsert the basket and press START/PAUSE to resume cooking.
11. When the Zone 1 timer reads 5 minutes, press START/PAUSE. Remove the basket. Spoon half of the mojo sauce over the tilapia. Reinsert the basket and press START/PAUSE to resume cooking.
12. When cooking is complete, the fish should be cooked through and the plantains crispy. Serve the tilapia and plantains with the remaining mojo sauce for dipping.

Parmesan-Crusted Fish Sticks with Baked Macaroni and Cheese

Prep time: 10 minutes, plus 5 minutes to stand | Cook time: 25 minutes | Serves 4

- For the fish sticks
- 1 pound cod or haddock fillets
- ½ cup all-purpose flour
- 2 large eggs
- ¼ teaspoon kosher salt
- ¼ teaspoon freshly ground black pepper
- ¾ cup panko bread crumbs
- ¼ cup grated Parmesan cheese
- Nonstick cooking spray
- For the macaroni and cheese
- 1½ cups elbow macaroni
- 1 cup whole milk
- 8 ounces shredded Colby-Jack cheese
- 4 ounces cream cheese, at room temperature
- 1 teaspoon Dijon mustard
- ½ teaspoon kosher salt
- ½ teaspoon freshly ground black pepper

1. To prep the fish sticks: Cut the fish into sticks about 3 inches long and ¾ inch wide.
2. Set up a breading station with three small shallow bowls. Place the flour in the first bowl. In the second bowl, whisk the eggs and season with the salt and black pepper. Combine the panko and Parmesan in the third bowl.
3. Bread the fish sticks in this order: First, dip them into the flour, coating all sides. Then, dip into the beaten egg. Finally, coat them in the panko mixture, gently pressing the bread crumbs into the fish. Spritz each fish stick all over with cooking spray.
4. To prep the macaroni and cheese: Place the macaroni in the Zone 2 basket. Add the milk, cream, Colby-Jack, cream cheese, mustard, salt, and black pepper. Stir well to combine, ensuring the pasta is completely submerged in the liquid.
5. To cook the fish sticks and macaroni and cheese: Install a crisper plate in the Zone 1 basket. Arrange the fish sticks in a single layer in the basket (use a rack or cook in batches if necessary) and insert the basket in the unit. Insert the Zone 2 basket in the unit.
6. Select Zone 1, select AIR FRY, set the temperature to 390°F, and set the timer to 18 minutes.
7. Select Zone 2, select BAKE, set the temperature to 360°F, and set the timer to 25 minutes. Select SMART FINISH.
8. Press START/PAUSE to begin cooking.
9. When the Zone 1 timer reads 3 minutes, press START/PAUSE. Remove the basket and use silicone-tipped tongs to gently flip over the fish sticks. Reinsert the basket and press START/PAUSE to resume cooking.
10. When cooking is complete, the fish sticks should be crisp and the macaroni tender.
11. Stir the macaroni cheese and let stand for 5 minutes before serving. The sauce will thicken as it cools.

Garlic Shrimp with Pasta Alfredo

Prep time: 10 minutes | Cook time: 40 minutes | Serves 4

- For the garlic shrimp
- 1 pound peeled small shrimp, thawed if frozen
- 1 tablespoon olive oil
- 1 tablespoon minced garlic
- ¼ teaspoon sea salt
- ¼ cup chopped fresh parsley
- For the pasta Alfredo
- 8 ounces no-boil lasagna noodles
- 2 cups whole milk
- ¼ cup heavy (whipping) cream
- 2 tablespoons unsalted butter, cut into small pieces
- 1 tablespoon minced garlic
- ½ teaspoon kosher salt
- ¼ teaspoon freshly ground black pepper
- ½ cup grated Parmesan cheese

1. To prep the garlic shrimp: In a large bowl, combine the shrimp, oil, garlic, and salt.
2. To prep the pasta alfredo: Break the lasagna noodles into 2-inch pieces. Add the milk to the Zone 2 basket, then add the noodles, cream, butter, garlic, salt, and black pepper. Stir well and ensure the pasta is fully submerged in the liquid.
3. To cook the shrimp and pasta: Install a crisper plate in the Zone 1 basket. Place the shrimp in the basket and insert the basket in the unit. Insert the Zone 2 basket in the unit.
4. Select Zone 1, select AIR FRY, set the temperature to 390°F, and set the timer to 13 minutes.
5. Select Zone 2, select BAKE, set the temperature to 360°F, and set the timer to 40 minutes. Select SMART FINISH.
6. Press START/PAUSE to begin cooking.
7. When the Zone 2 timer reads 20 minutes, press START/PAUSE. Remove the basket and stir the pasta. Reinsert the basket and press START/PAUSE to resume cooking.
8. When cooking is complete, the shrimp will be cooked through and the pasta tender.
9. Transfer the pasta to a serving dish and stir in the Parmesan. Top with the shrimp and parsley.

Pecan-Crusted Catfish Nuggets with "Fried" Okra

Prep time: 15 minutes, plus 1 hour to soak | Cook time: 17 minutes | Serves 4

- For the catfish nuggets
- 1 cup whole milk
- 1 pound fresh catfish nuggets (or cut-up fillets)
- 1 large egg
- 2 to 3 dashes Louisiana-style hot sauce (optional)
- ¼ cup finely chopped pecans
- ½ cup all-purpose flour
- Nonstick cooking spray
- Tartar sauce, for serving (optional)
- For the okra
- ½ cup fine yellow cornmeal
- ¼ cup all-purpose flour
- ½ teaspoon garlic powder
- ½ teaspoon paprika
- 1 teaspoon kosher salt
- 1 large egg
- 8 ounces frozen cut okra, thawed
- Nonstick cooking spray

1. To prep the catfish: Pour the milk into a large zip-top bag. Add the catfish and turn to coat. Set in the refrigerator to soak for at least 1 hour or up to overnight.
2. Remove the fish from the milk, shaking off any excess liquid.
3. In a shallow dish, whisk together the egg and hot sauce (if using). In a second shallow dish, combine the pecans and flour.
4. Dip each piece of fish into the egg mixture, then into the nut mixture to coat. Gently press the nut mixture to adhere to the fish. Spritz each nugget with cooking spray.
5. To prep the okra: Set up a breading station with two small shallow bowls. In the first bowl, stir together the cornmeal, flour, garlic powder, paprika, and salt. In the second bowl, whisk the egg.
6. Dip the okra first in the cornmeal mixture, then the egg, then back into the cornmeal. Spritz with cooking spray.
7. To cook the catfish and okra: Install a crisper plate in each of the two baskets. Place the fish in a single layer in the Zone 1 basket and insert the basket in the unit. Place the okra in the Zone 2 basket and insert the basket in the unit.
8. Select Zone 1, select AIR FRY, set the temperature to 390°F, and set the timer to 17 minutes.
9. Select Zone 2, select AIR FRY, set the temperature to 400°F, and set the timer to 12 minutes. Select SMART FINISH.
10. Press START/PAUSE to begin cooking.
11. When cooking is complete, the fish should be cooked through and the okra golden brown and crispy. Serve hot.

"Fried" Fish with Seasoned Potato Wedges

Prep time: 10 minutes, plus 10 minutes to rest | Cook time: 30 minutes | Serves 4

- For the fish
- 4 cod fillets (6 ounces each)
- 4 tablespoons all-purpose flour, divided
- ¼ cup cornstarch
- 1 teaspoon baking powder
- ¼ teaspoon kosher salt
- ⅓ cup lager-style beer or sparkling water
- Tartar sauce, cocktail sauce, or malt vinegar, for serving (optional)
- For the potatoes
- 4 russet potatoes
- 2 tablespoons vegetable oil
- ½ teaspoon paprika
- ½ teaspoon kosher salt
- ¼ teaspoon garlic powder
- ¼ teaspoon freshly ground black pepper

1. To prep the fish: Pat the fish dry with a paper towel and coat lightly with 2 tablespoons of flour.
2. In a shallow dish, combine the remaining 2 tablespoons of flour, the cornstarch, baking powder, and salt. Stir in the beer to form a thick batter.
3. Dip the fish in the batter to coat both sides, then let rest on a cutting board for 10 minutes.
4. To prep the potatoes: Cut each potato in half lengthwise, then cut each half into 4 wedges.
5. In a large bowl, combine the potatoes and oil. Toss well to fully coat the potatoes. Add the paprika, salt, garlic powder, and black pepper and toss well to coat.
6. To cook the fish and potato wedges: Install a crisper plate in each of the two baskets. Place a piece of parchment paper or aluminum foil over the plate in the Zone 1 basket. Place the fish in the basket and insert the basket in the unit. Place the potato wedges in a single layer in the Zone 2 basket and insert the basket in the unit.
7. Select Zone 1, select AIR FRY, set the temperature to 400°F, and set the timer to 13 minutes.
8. Select Zone 2, select AIR FRY, set the temperature to 400°F, and set the timer to 30 minutes. Select SMART FINISH.
9. Press START/PAUSE to begin cooking.
10. When the Zone 1 timer reads 5 minutes, press START/PAUSE. Remove the basket and use a silicone spatula to carefully flip the fish over. Reinsert the basket and press START/PAUSE to resume cooking.
11. When cooking is complete, the fish should be cooked through and the potatoes crispy outside and tender inside. Serve hot with tartar sauce, cocktail sauce, or malt vinegar (if using).

Shrimp Po'Boys with Sweet Potato Fries

Prep time: 20 minutes, plus 10 minutes to sit | Cook time: 30 minutes | Serves 4

- For the shrimp po'boys
- ½ cup buttermilk
- 1 tablespoon Louisiana-style hot sauce
- ¾ cup all-purpose flour
- ½ cup cornmeal
- ½ teaspoon kosher salt
- ½ teaspoon paprika
- ½ teaspoon garlic powder
- ½ teaspoon freshly ground black pepper
- 1 pound peeled medium shrimp, thawed if frozen
- Nonstock cooking spray
- ½ cup store-bought rémoulade sauce
- 4 French bread rolls, halved lengthwise
- ½ cup shredded lettuce
- 1 tomato, sliced
- For the sweet potato fries
- 2 medium sweet potatoes
- 2 teaspoons vegetable oil
- ¼ teaspoon garlic powder
- ¼ teaspoon paprika
- ¼ teaspoon kosher salt

1. To prep the shrimp: In a medium bowl, combine the buttermilk and hot sauce. In a shallow bowl, combine the flour, cornmeal, salt, paprika, garlic powder, and black pepper.
2. Add the shrimp to the buttermilk and stir to coat. Remove the shrimp, letting the excess buttermilk drip off, then add to the cornmeal mixture to coat.
3. Spritz the breaded shrimp with cooking spray, then let sit for 10 minutes.
4. To prep the sweet potatoes: Peel the sweet potatoes and cut them lengthwise into ¼-inch-thick sticks (like shoestring fries).
5. In a large bowl, combine the sweet potatoes, oil, garlic powder, paprika, and salt. Toss to coat.
6. To cook the shrimp and fries: Install a crisper plate in each of the two baskets. Place the shrimp in the Zone 1 basket and insert the basket in the unit. Place the sweet potatoes in a single layer in the Zone 2 basket and insert the basket in the unit.
7. Select Zone 1, select AIR FRY, set the temperature to 390°F, and set the timer to 13 minutes.
8. Select Zone 2, select AIR FRY, set the temperature to 400°F, and set the timer to 30 minutes. Select SMART FINISH.
9. Press START/PAUSE to begin cooking.
10. When cooking is complete, the shrimp should be golden and cooked through and the sweet potato fries crisp.
11. Spread the rémoulade on the cut sides of the rolls. Divide the lettuce and tomato among the rolls, then top with the fried shrimp. Serve with the sweet potato fries on the side.

Broiled Crab Cakes with Hush Puppies

Prep time: 20 minutes, plus 30 minutes to chill | Cook time: 15 minutes | Serves 4

- For the crab cakes
- 2 large eggs
- 2 tablespoons Dijon mustard
- 2 teaspoons Worcestershire sauce
- 1 teaspoon Old Bay seasoning
- ¼ teaspoon paprika
- ¼ cup cracker crumbs (about 9 crackers)
- 1 pound lump crab meat
- 2 teaspoons vegetable oil
- For the hush puppies
- ½ cup all-purpose flour
- ⅓ cup yellow cornmeal
- 3 tablespoons sugar
- ¼ teaspoon kosher salt
- ¼ teaspoon baking powder
- 1 large egg
- ½ cup whole milk
- Nonstick cooking spray

1. To prep the crab cakes: In a large bowl, whisk together the eggs, mustard, Worcestershire, Old Bay, and paprika until smooth. Stir in the cracker crumbs until fully incorporated, then fold in the crab meat. Refrigerate the crab mixture for 30 minutes.
2. Divide the crab mixture into 8 equal portions. With damp hands, press each portion gently into a loose patty. Brush both sides of each patty with the oil.
3. To prep the hush puppies: In a large bowl, combine the flour, cornmeal, sugar, salt, and baking powder. Stir in the egg and milk to form a stiff batter.
4. Roll the batter into 8 balls. Spritz each hush puppy with cooking spray.
5. To cook the crab cakes and hush puppies: Install a crisper plate in each of the two baskets. Place the crab cakes in a single layer in the Zone 1 basket and insert the basket in the unit. Line the Zone 2 plate with aluminum foil and spray the foil with cooking spray. Arrange the hush puppies on the foil and insert the basket in the unit.
6. Select Zone 1, select AIR BROIL, set the temperature to 400°F, and set the timer to 15 minutes.
7. Select Zone 2, select AIR FRY, set the temperature to 400°F, and set the timer to 7 minutes. Select SMART FINISH.
8. Press START/PAUSE to begin cooking.
9. When cooking is complete, the crab cakes and hush puppies will be golden brown and cooked through. Serve hot.

Chapter 7
Vegetables and Side Dishes Recipes

Simple Green Beans

Prep time: 5 minutes | Cook time: 7 minutes | Serves 4

- 1 pound (454 g) fresh green beans, cleaned and trimmed
- ½ teaspoon garlic powder
- ½ teaspoon cumin powder
- ½ teaspoon onion powder
- ½ teaspoon dried dill weed
- 1 teaspoon olive oil
- Sea salt and red pepper flakes, to taste

1. Start by preheating the air fryer to 375°F (190°C).
2. Toss the green beans with the remaining ingredients until they are well coated.
3. Arrange the green beans in the crisper tray.
4. Place the crisper tray in the corresponding position in the air fryer. Select Air Fry and cook the green beans for 7 minutes; make sure to check the green beans halfway through the cooking time.
5. Taste, adjust the seasonings, and serve warm. Bon appétit!

Broccoli with Garlic

Prep time: 5 minutes | Cook time: 6 minutes | Serves 3

- ¾ pound (340 g) broccoli florets
- 1 tablespoon olive oil
- 1 teaspoon garlic powder
- Sea salt and ground black pepper, to taste

1. Start by preheating the air fryer to 395°F (202°C).
2. Toss the broccoli florets with the remaining ingredients until well coated.
3. Arrange the broccoli florets in the crisper tray.
4. Place the crisper tray in the corresponding position in the air fryer. Select Air Fry and cook the broccoli florets for 6 minutes, shaking crisper tray halfway through the cooking time.
5. Bon appétit!

Creamy Cauliflower Salad with Bacon

Prep time: 5 minutes | Cook time: 12 minutes | Serves 3

- ¾ pound (340 g) cauliflower florets
- 2 ounces (57 g) bacon, diced
- ¼ cup sour cream
- ¼ cup mayonnaise
- 1 teaspoon Dijon mustard
- 1 tablespoon apple cider vinegar
- 1 garlic clove, minced
- 1 small red onion, thinly sliced
- Kosher salt and freshly ground black pepper, to taste

1. Start by preheating the air fryer to 400°F (205°C).
2. Place the cauliflower florets in a lightly greased crisper tray.
3. Place the crisper tray in the corresponding position in the air fryer. Select Air Fry and cook the cauliflower florets for 12 minutes, shaking crisper tray halfway through the cooking time.
4. Thoroughly combine the cauliflower florets with the remaining ingredients. Serve well chilled and enjoy!

Fried Patty Pan Squash

Prep time: 10 minutes | Cook time: 15 minutes | Serves 6

- 5 cups small pattypan squash, halved
- 1 tablespoon olive oil
- 2 garlic cloves, minced
- ½ teaspoon salt
- ¼ teaspoon dried oregano
- ¼ teaspoon dried thyme
- ¼ teaspoon pepper
- 1 tablespoon minced parsley

1. Rub the squash with oil, garlic and the rest of the ingredients.
2. Spread the squash in the air fryer baskets.
3. Return the air fryer basket 1 to Zone 1, and basket 2 to Zone 2 of the Ninja Foodi 2-Basket Air Fryer.
4. Choose the "Air Fry" mode for Zone 1 at 375 degrees F and 15 minutes of cooking time.
5. Select the "MATCH COOK" option to copy the settings for Zone 2.
6. Initiate cooking by pressing the START/PAUSE BUTTON.
7. Flip the squash once cooked halfway through.
8. Garnish with parsley.
9. Serve warm.

Acorn Squash Slices

Prep time: 15 minutes | Cook time: 10 minutes | Serves 6

- 2 medium acorn squashes
- ⅔ cup packed brown sugar
- ½ cup butter, melted

1. Cut the squash in half, remove the seeds and slice into ½ inch slices.
2. Place the squash slices in the air fryer baskets.
3. Drizzle brown sugar and butter over the squash slices.
4. Return the air fryer basket 1 to Zone 1, and basket 2 to Zone 2 of the Ninja Foodi 2-Basket Air Fryer.
5. Choose the "Air Fry" mode for Zone 1 and set the temperature to 350 degrees F and 10 minutes of cooking time.
6. Select the "MATCH COOK" option to copy the settings for Zone 2.
7. Initiate cooking by pressing the START/PAUSE BUTTON.
8. Flip the squash once cooked halfway through.
9. Serve.

Green Tomato Stacks

Prep time: 15 minutes | Cook time: 12 minutes | Serves 6

- ¼ cup mayonnaise
- ¼ teaspoon lime zest, grated
- 2 tablespoons lime juice
- 1 teaspoon minced fresh thyme
- ½ teaspoon black pepper
- ¼ cup all-purpose flour
- 2 large egg whites, beaten
- ¾ cup cornmeal
- ¼ teaspoon salt
- 2 medium green tomatoes
- 2 medium re tomatoes
- Cooking spray
- 8 slices Canadian bacon, warmed

1. Mix mayonnaise with ¼ teaspoon black pepper, thyme, lime juice and zest in a bowl.
2. Spread flour in one bowl, beat egg whites in another bowl and mix cornmeal with ¼ teaspoon black pepper and salt in a third bowl.
3. Cut the tomatoes into 4 slices and coat each with the flour then dip in the egg whites.
4. Coat the tomatoes slices with the cornmeal mixture.
5. Place the slices in the air fryer baskets.
6. Return the air fryer basket 1 to Zone 1, and basket 2 to Zone 2 of the Ninja Foodi 2-Basket Air Fryer.
7. Choose the "Air Fry" mode for Zone 1 at 390 degrees F and 12 minutes of cooking time.
8. Select the "MATCH COOK" option to copy the settings for Zone 2.
9. Initiate cooking by pressing the START/PAUSE BUTTON.
10. Flip the tomatoes once cooked halfway through.
11. Place the green tomato slices on the working surface.
12. Top them with bacon, and red tomato slice.
13. Serve.

Healthy Air Fried Veggies

Prep time: 10 minutes | Cook time: 15 minutes | Serves 4

- 52g onion, sliced
- 71g broccoli florets
- 116g radishes, sliced
- 15ml olive oil
- 100g Brussels sprouts, cut in half
- 325g cauliflower florets
- 1 tsp balsamic vinegar
- ½ tsp garlic powder
- Pepper
- Salt

1. In a bowl, toss veggies with oil, vinegar, garlic powder, pepper, and salt.
2. Insert a crisper plate in the Ninja Foodi air fryer baskets.
3. Add veggies in both baskets.
4. Select zone 1 then select "air fry" mode and set the temperature to 380 degrees F for 15 minutes. Press "match" to match zone 2 settings to zone 1. Press "start/stop" to begin. Stir halfway through.

Bacon Wrapped Corn Cob

Prep time: 15 minutes | Cook time: 10 minutes | Serves 4

- 4 trimmed corns on the cob
- 8 bacon slices

1. Wrap the corn cobs with two bacon slices.
2. Place the wrapped cobs into the Ninja Foodi 2 Baskets Air Fryer baskets.
3. Return the air fryer basket 1 to Zone 1, and basket 2 to Zone 2 of the Ninja Foodi 2-Basket Air Fryer.
4. Choose the "Air Fry" mode for Zone 1 and set the temperature to 355 degrees F and 10 minutes of cooking time.
5. Select the "MATCH COOK" option to copy the settings for Zone 2.
6. Initiate cooking by pressing the START/PAUSE BUTTON.
7. Flip the corn cob once cooked halfway through.
8. Serve warm.

Cauliflower with Onion

Prep time: 5 minutes | Cook time: 13 minutes | Serves 3

- ¾ pound (340 g) cauliflower florets
- 1 large onion, cut into wedges
- 2 cloves garlic, pressed
- 1 tablespoon olive oil
- Sea salt and ground black pepper, to taste
- 1 teaspoon paprika

1. Start by preheating the air fryer to 400°F (205°C).
2. Toss the cauliflower florets and onion with the garlic, olive oil, and spices. Toss until they are well coated on all sides.
3. Arrange the vegetables in the crisper tray.
4. Place the crisper tray in the corresponding position in the air fryer. Select Air Fry and cook the vegetables for about 13 minutes, shaking crisper tray halfway through the cooking time.
5. Bon appétit!

Buffalo Bites

Prep time: 10 minutes | Cook time: 30 minutes | Serves 6

FOR THE BITES:

- 1 small cauliflower head, cut into florets
- 2 tablespoons olive oil
- 3 tablespoons buffalo wing sauce
- 3 tablespoons butter, melted
- For the dip:
- 1½ cups 2% cottage cheese
- ¼ cup fat-free plain Greek yogurt
- ¼ cup crumbled blue cheese
- 1 sachet ranch salad dressing mix
- Celery sticks (optional)

1. In a large bowl, combine the cauliflower and oil| toss to coat.
2. Place a crisper plate in each drawer. Put the coated cauliflower florets in each drawer in a single layer. Place the drawers in the unit.
3. Select zone 1, then AIR FRY, then set the temperature to 360 degrees F/ 180 degrees C with a 15-minute timer. To match zone 2 settings to zone 1, choose MATCH. To begin, select START/ STOP.
4. Remove the cauliflower from the drawers after the timer has finished.
5. Combine the buffalo sauce and melted butter in a large mixing bowl. Put in the cauliflower and toss to coat. Place on a serving dish and serve.
6. Combine the dip ingredients in a small bowl. Serve with the cauliflower and celery sticks, if desired.

Breaded Summer Squash

Prep time: 15 minutes | Cook time: 10 minutes | Serves 4

- 4 cups yellow summer squash, sliced
- 3 tablespoons olive oil
- ½ teaspoon salt
- ½ teaspoon pepper
- ⅛ teaspoon cayenne pepper
- ¾ cup panko bread crumbs
- ¾ cup grated Parmesan cheese

1. Mix crumbs, cheese, cayenne pepper, black pepper, salt and oil in a bowl.
2. Coat the squash slices with the breadcrumb mixture.
3. Place these slices in the air fryer baskets.
4. Return the air fryer basket 1 to Zone 1, and basket 2 to Zone 2 of the Ninja Foodi 2-Basket Air Fryer.
5. Choose the "Air Fry" mode for Zone 1 at 350 degrees F and 10 minutes of cooking time.
6. Select the "MATCH COOK" option to copy the settings for Zone 2.
7. Initiate cooking by pressing the START/PAUSE BUTTON.
8. Flip the squash slices once cooked half way through.
9. Serve warm.

Beet Salad

Prep time: 5 minutes | Cook time: 40 minutes | Serves 4

- 1 pound (454 g) beets
- ½ teaspoon cumin seeds
- Sea salt and red pepper flakes, to taste
- 2 tablespoons apple cider vinegar
- 4 tablespoons olive oil
- 1 teaspoon crushed garlic

1. Start by preheating the air fryer to 400°F (205°C).
2. Arrange the beets in the crisper tray.
3. Place the crisper tray in the corresponding position in the air fryer. Select Air Fry and cook the beets for 40 minutes, shaking crisper tray halfway through the cooking time. Let them cool completely.
4. Peel the beets and cut them into thin slices; transfer to a salad bowl. Add in the remaining ingredients and stir to combine.
5. Bon appétit!

Fried Asparagus

Prep time: 5 minutes | Cook time: 6 minutes | Serves 4

- ¼ cup mayonnaise
- 4 teaspoons olive oil
- 1½ teaspoons grated lemon zest
- 1 garlic clove, minced
- ½ teaspoon pepper
- ¼ teaspoon seasoned salt
- 1-pound fresh asparagus, trimmed
- 2 tablespoons shredded parmesan cheese
- Lemon wedges (optional)

1. In a large bowl, combine the first 6 ingredients.
2. Add the asparagus| toss to coat.
3. Put a crisper plate in both drawers. Put the asparagus in a single layer in each drawer. Top with the parmesan cheese. Place the drawers into the unit.
4. Select zone 1, then AIR FRY, then set the temperature to 375 degrees F/ 190 degrees C with a 6-minute timer. To match zone 2 settings to zone 1, choose MATCH. To begin, select START/STOP.
5. Remove the asparagus from the drawers after the timer has finished.

Air-Fried Radishes

Prep time: 10 minutes | Cook time: 15 minutes | Serves 6

- 1020g radishes, quartered
- 3 tablespoons olive oil
- 1 tablespoon fresh oregano, minced
- ¼ teaspoon salt
- ⅛ teaspoon black pepper

1. Toss radishes with oil, black pepper, salt and oregano in a bowl.
2. Divide the radishes into the Ninja Foodi 2 Baskets Air Fryer baskets.
3. Return the air fryer basket 1 to Zone 1, and basket 2 to Zone 2 of the Ninja Foodi 2-Basket Air Fryer.
4. Choose the "Air Fry" mode for Zone 1 at 375 degrees F and 15 minutes of cooking time.
5. Select the "MATCH COOK" option to copy the settings for Zone 2.
6. Initiate cooking by pressing the START/PAUSE BUTTON.
7. Toss the radishes once cooked halfway through.
8. Serve.

Garlic Herb Radishes

Prep time: 10 minutes | Cook time: 10 minutes | Serves 4

- 450 g radishes
- 2 tablespoons unsalted butter, melted
- ½ teaspoon garlic powder
- ½ teaspoon dried parsley
- ¼ teaspoon dried oregano
- ¼ teaspoon ground black pepper

1. Remove roots from radishes and cut into quarters.
2. In a small bowl, add butter and seasonings.
3. Toss the radishes in the herb butter and place into the zone 1 air fryer drawer.
4. Select Air Fryer button and adjust the temperature to 180°C and set the time to 10 minutes.
5. Halfway through the cooking time, toss the radishes in the air fryer drawer.
6. Continue cooking until edges begin to turn brown. Serve warm.

Sausage-Stuffed Mushroom Caps

Prep time: 10 minutes | Cook time: 8 minutes | Serves 2

- 6 large portobello mushroom caps
- 230 g Italian sausage
- 15 g chopped onion
- 2 tablespoons blanched finely ground almond flour
- 20 g grated Parmesan cheese
- 1 teaspoon minced fresh garlic

1. Use a spoon to hollow out each mushroom cap, reserving scrapings.
2. In a medium skillet over medium heat, brown the sausage about 10 minutes or until fully cooked and no pink remains.
3. Drain and then add reserved mushroom scrapings, onion, almond flour, Parmesan, and garlic.
4. Gently fold ingredients together and continue cooking an additional minute, then remove from heat.
5. Evenly spoon the mixture into mushroom caps and place the caps into a 6-inch round pan.
6. Place pan into the zone 1 air fryer drawer. Select Air Fry button and adjust the temperature to 192°C and set the time to 8 minutes.
7. When finished cooking, the tops will be browned and bubbling. Serve warm.

Roasted Aubergine

Prep time: 15 minutes | Cook time: 15 minutes | Serves 4

- 1 large aubergine
- 2 tablespoons olive oil
- ¼ teaspoon salt
- ½ teaspoon garlic powder

1. Remove top and bottom from aubergine. Slice aubergine into ¼-inch-thick round slices.
2. Brush slices with olive oil. Sprinkle with salt and garlic powder.
3. Place aubergine slices into the zone 1 air fryer drawer. Select Roast button and adjust the temperature to 200°C and set the time to 15 minutes.
4. Serve immediately.

Homemade Potato

Prep time: 5 minutes | Cook time: 20 minutes | Serves 3

- ¾ pound (340 g) fingerling potatoes
- 1 tablespoon olive oil
- ½ teaspoon onion powder
- 1 teaspoon garlic powder
- 1 teaspoon chili pepper
- Sea salt and ground black pepper, to taste

1. Start by preheating the air fryer to 400°F (205°C).
2. Toss the potatoes with the remaining ingredients until well coated on all sides.
3. Arrange the potatoes in the crisper tray.
4. Place the crisper tray in the corresponding position in the air fryer. Select Air Fry and cook the potatoes for about 20 minutes, shaking crisper tray halfway through the cooking time.
5. Garnish with fresh or dried herbs, if desired. Bon appétit!

Stuffed Tomatoes

Prep time: 12 minutes | Cook time: 8 minutes | Serves 2

- 2 cups brown rice, cooked
- 1 cup tofu, grilled and chopped
- 4 large red tomatoes
- 4 tablespoons basil, chopped
- ¼ tablespoon olive oil
- Salt and black pepper, to taste
- 2 tablespoons lemon juice
- 1 teaspoon red chili powder
- ½ cup Parmesan cheese

1. Take a large bowl and mix rice, tofu, basil, olive oil, salt, black pepper, lemon juice, and chili powder.
2. Core the center of the tomatoes.
3. Fill the cavity with the rice mixture.
4. Top them off with the cheese sprinkle.
5. Divide the tomatoes into two air fryer baskets.
6. Turn zone 1 to AIR FRY mode for 8 minutes at 400 degrees F/ 200 degrees C.
7. Select the MATCH button for zone 2.
8. Serve and enjoy.

Butter Brussels Sprouts

Prep time: 5 minutes | Cook time: 14 minutes | Serves 3

- ¾ pound (340 g) Brussels sprouts
- 2 tablespoons butter, melted
- 2 garlic cloves, crushed
- Kosher salt and ground black pepper, to taste

1. Start by preheating the air fryer to 380°F (193°C).
2. Toss the Brussels sprouts with the remaining ingredients until well coated.
3. Arrange the Brussels sprouts in the crisper tray.
4. Place the crisper tray in the corresponding position in the air fryer. Select Air Fry and cook the Brussels sprouts for 14 minutes, shaking crisper tray halfway through the cooking time.
5. Bon appétit!

Air Fried Mushrooms

Prep time: 8 minutes | Cook time: 11 minutes | Serves 3

- ¾ pound (340 g) button mushrooms, cleaned and cut into halves
- 2 tablespoons olive oil
- 1 garlic clove, pressed
- Sea salt and ground black pepper, to taste
- 1 tablespoon fresh lemon juice
- 1 tablespoon chopped fresh cilantro

1. Start by preheating the air fryer to 375°F (190°C).
2. Toss the mushrooms with the olive oil, garlic, salt, and black pepper.
3. Arrange them in a lightly oiled crisper tray.
4. Place the crisper tray in the corresponding position in the air fryer. Select Air Fry and cook the mushrooms for about 11 minutes, shaking crisper tray halfway through the cooking time.
5. Drizzle fresh lemon juice over the mushroom and serve with the fresh cilantro. Enjoy

Easy Eggplant

Prep time: 10 minutes | Cook time: 15 minutes | Serves 3

- ¾ pound (340 g) eggplant, peeled and diced
- 2 tablespoons sesame oil
- ½ teaspoon cumin powder
- ½ teaspoon onion powder
- 1 teaspoon granulated garlic

1. Start by preheating the air fryer to 400°F (205°C).
2. Toss the eggplant pieces with the remaining ingredients until they are well coated on all sides.
3. Arrange the eggplant in the crisper tray.
4. Place the crisper tray in the corresponding position in the air fryer. Select Air Fry and cook the eggplant for about 15 minutes, shaking crisper tray halfway through the cooking time.
5. Garnish with fresh herbs, if desired. Bon appétit!

Yellow Beans with Tomato

Prep time: 5 minutes | Cook time: 8 minutes | Serves 3

- ½ pound (227 g) yellow beans, trimmed
- 2 small tomatoes, sliced
- 1 tablespoon sesame oil
- Sea salt and ground black pepper, to taste

1. Start by preheating the air fryer to 390°F (199°C).
2. Toss the yellow beans and tomatoes with the sesame oil, salt, and black pepper; toss until they are well coated.
3. Arrange the vegetables in the crisper tray.
4. Place the crisper tray in the corresponding position in the air fryer. Select Air Fry and cook the vegetables for 8 minutes; make sure to stir the vegetables halfway through the cooking time.
5. Taste, adjust the seasonings, and serve immediately. Bon appétit!

Chapter 8
Snack Recipes

Prosciutto Mozzarella Bites

Prep time: 5 minutes |Cook time: 6 minutes | Serves 8

- 8 pieces full-fat mozzarella string cheese
- 8 thin slices prosciutto
- 16 basil leaves

1. Preheat the air fryer to 360°F.
2. Cut the string cheese in half across the center, not lengthwise. Do the same with the prosciutto.
3. Place a piece of prosciutto onto a clean workspace. Top the prosciutto with a basil leaf and then a piece of string cheese. Roll up the string cheese inside the prosciutto and secure with a wooden toothpick. Repeat with the remaining cheese sticks.
4. Place the prosciutto mozzarella bites into the air fryer basket and cook for 6 minutes, checking for doneness at 4 minutes.

Muffuletta Sliders

Prep time: 5 minutes |Cook time: 7 minutes | Serves 8

- ¼ pound thin-sliced deli ham
- ¼ pound thin-sliced pastrami
- 4 ounces low-fat mozzarella cheese, grated or sliced thin
- 8 slider buns
- olive oil for misting
- 1 tablespoon sesame seeds
- Olive Mix
- ¼ cup sliced black olives
- ½ cup sliced green olives with pimentos
- ¼ cup chopped kalamata olives
- 1 teaspoon red wine vinegar
- ¼ teaspoon basil
- ⅛ teaspoon garlic powder

1. In a small bowl, stir together all the Olive Mix ingredients.
2. Divide the meats and cheese into 8 equal portions. To assemble sliders, stack in this order: bottom bun, ham, pastrami, 2 tablespoons olive mix, cheese, top bun.
3. Mist tops of sliders lightly with oil. Sprinkle with sesame seeds.
4. Cooking 4 at a time, place sliders in air fryer basket and cook at 360°F for 7 minutes to melt cheese and heat through.

Parmesan Eggplant Bites

Prep time: 5 minutes |Cook time: 35 minutes | Serves 4

- 2 eggs
- 2 tbsp heavy cream
- ½ cup bread crumbs
- ½ tsp Italian seasoning
- ½ cup grated Parmesan
- ½ tsp salt
- 1 eggplant, cut into sticks
- ½ cup tomato sauce, warm

1. Preheat air fryer to 400°F. In a bowl, mix the eggs and heavy cream. In another bowl, combine bread crumbs, Parmesan cheese, Italian seasoning and salt. Dip eggplant fries in egg mixture and dredge them in crumb mixture.
2. Place the fries in the greased frying basket and Air Fry for 12 minutes, shaking once. Transfer to a large serving plate and serve with warmed tomato sauce.

Savory Sausage Balls

Cook time: 8 minutes | Serves 10

- 2 cups all-purpose flour
- 1 tablespoon baking powder
- ½ teaspoon garlic powder
- ¼ teaspoon onion powder
- ½ teaspoon salt
- 3 tablespoons milk
- 2½ cups grated pepper jack cheese
- 1 pound fresh sausage, casing removed

1. Preheat the air fryer to 370°F.
2. In a large bowl, whisk together the flour, baking powder, garlic powder, onion powder, and salt. Add in the milk, grated cheese, and sausage.
3. Using a tablespoon, scoop out the sausage and roll it between your hands to form a rounded ball. You should end up with approximately 32 balls. Place them in the air fryer basket in a single layer and working in batches as necessary.
4. Cook for 8 minutes, or until the outer coating turns light brown.
5. Carefully remove, repeating with the remaining sausage balls.

Hot Nachos with Chile Salsa

Prep time: 5 minutes |Cook time: 20 minutes | Serves 4

- ½ chile de árbol pepper, seeds removed
- 1 tbsp olive oil
- Salt to taste
- 1 shallot, chopped
- 2 garlic cloves
- 1 can diced tomatoes
- 2 tbsp fresh cilantro
- Juice of 1 lime
- ¼ tsp chili-lime seasoning
- 6 corn tortillas

1. Add the shallot, garlic, chile de árbol, tomatoes, cilantro, lime juice and salt in a food processor. Pulse until combined and chunky. Pour the salsa into a serving bowl and set aside. Drizzle olive oil on both sides of the tortillas. Stack the tortilla and cut them in half with a sharp knife. Continue to cut into quarters, then cut again so that each tortilla is cut into 8 equal wedges. Season both sides of each wedge with chile-lime seasoning.
2. Preheat air fryer to 400°F. Place the tortilla wedges in the greased frying basket and Air Fry for 4-7 minutes, shaking once until the chips are golden and crisp. Allow to cool slightly and serve with previously prepared salsa.

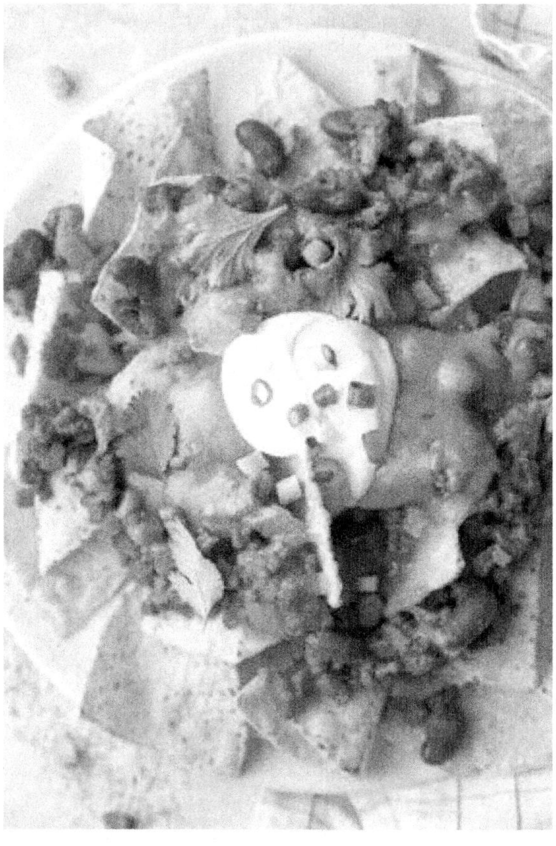

Pork Pot Stickers with Yum Yum Sauce

Prep time: 5 minutes |Cook time: 8 minutes | Serves 48

- 1 pound ground pork
- 2 cups shredded green cabbage
- ¼ cup shredded carrot
- ½ cup finely chopped water chestnuts
- 2 teaspoons minced fresh ginger
- ¼ cup hoisin sauce
- 2 tablespoons soy sauce
- 1 tablespoon sesame oil
- freshly ground black pepper
- 3 scallions, minced
- 48 round dumpling wrappers (or wonton wrappers with the corners cut off to make them round)
- 1 tablespoon vegetable oil
- Yum Yum Sauce:
- 1½ cups mayonnaise
- 3 tablespoons rice vinegar
- 1 teaspoon soy sauce
- 2 tablespoons ketchup
- 1½ teaspoons paprika
- ¼ teaspoon ground cayenne pepper
- ¼ teaspoon garlic powder

1. Preheat a large sauté pan over medium-high heat. Add the ground pork and brown for a few minutes. Remove the cooked pork to a bowl using a slotted spoon and discard the fat from the pan. Return the cooked pork to the sauté pan and add the cabbage, carrots and water chestnuts. Sauté for a minute and then add the fresh ginger, hoisin sauce, soy sauce, sesame oil, and freshly ground black pepper. Sauté for a few more minutes, just until cabbage and carrots are soft. Then stir in the scallions and transfer the pork filling to a bowl to cool.
2. Make the pot stickers in batches of 1 Place 12 dumpling wrappers on a flat surface. Brush a little water around the perimeter of the wrappers. Place a rounded teaspoon of the filling into the center of each wrapper. Fold the wrapper over the filling, bringing the edges together to form a half moon, sealing the edges shut. Brush a little more water on the top surface of the sealed edge of the pot sticker. Make pleats in the dough around the sealed edge by pinching the dough and folding the edge over on itself. You should have about 5 to 6 pleats in the dough. Repeat this three times until you have 48 pot stickers. Freeze the pot stickers for 2 hours (or as long as 3 weeks in an airtight container).
3. Preheat the air fryer to 400°F.
4. Air-fry the pot stickers in batches of 16. Brush or spray the pot stickers with vegetable oil just before putting them in the air fryer basket. Air-fry for 8 minutes, turning the pot stickers once or twice during the cooking process.
5. While the pot stickers are cooking, combine all the ingredients for the Yum Yum sauce in a bowl. Serve the pot stickers warm with the Yum Yum sauce and soy sauce for dipping.

Herbed Cheese Brittle

Cook time: 5 minutes | Serves 4

- ½ cup shredded Parmesan cheese
- ½ cup shredded white cheddar cheese
- 1 tablespoon fresh chopped rosemary
- 1 teaspoon garlic powder
- 1 large egg white

1. Preheat the air fryer to 400°F.
2. In a large bowl, mix the cheeses, rosemary, and garlic powder. Mix in the egg white. Then pour the batter into a 7-inch pan (or an air-fryer-compatible pan).
3. Place the pan in the air fryer basket and cook for 4 to 5 minutes, or until the cheese is melted and slightly browned.
4. Remove the pan from the air fryer, and let it cool for 2 minutes. Invert the pan before the cheese brittle completely cools but is semi-hardened to allow it to easily slide out of the pan.
5. Let the pan cool another 5 minutes. Break into pieces and serve.

Mozzarella Sticks

Prep time: 10 minutes | Cook time: 6 minutes | Serves 6

- 150g block Mozzarella cheese or string cheese
- 6 slices of white bread
- 1 large egg
- 1 tablespoon water
- 55g panko breadcrumbs
- 1 tablespoon olive oil

1. Remove the crust from the bread. Discard or save for breadcrumbs.
2. Roll the bread into thin slices with a rolling pin.
3. Slice mozzarella into 30 cm x 10 cm -long sticks, nearly the same size as your bread slices.
4. In a small bowl, whisk together the egg and the water.
5. Fill a shallow pie plate halfway with panko.
6. Wrap a bread slice around each mozzarella stick.
7. Brush the egg wash around the edge of the bread and push to seal it. Brush all over the bread outside.
8. Dredge in Panko and push to coat on all sides.
9. Line basket with parchment paper.
10. Press either "Zone 1" or "Zone 2" and then rotate the knob to select "Air Fryer".
11. Set the temperature to 200 degrees C, and then set the time for 5 minutes to preheat.
12. After preheating, arrange sticks into the basket.
13. Slide the basket into the Air Fryer and set the time for 6 minutes.
14. After cooking time is completed, place on a wire rack for a few minutes, then transfer onto serving plates and serve.

Hot Garlic Kale Chips

Prep time: 5 minutes |Cook time: 20 minutes | Serves 6

- 1 tbsp chili powder
- 1 tsp garlic powder
- 6 cups kale, torn
- 3 tsp olive oil
- Sea salt to taste

1. Preheat air fryer to 390°F. Mix the garlic and chili powders. Coat the kale with olive oil, chili, and garlic powder. Put it in the frying basket and Air Fry until crispy, about 5-6 minutes, shaking the basket at around 3 minutes.
2. Toss some sea salt on the kale chips once they are finished and serve.

Cheesy Spinach Dip

Cook time: 35 minutes | Serves 6

- ½ can refrigerated breadstick dough
- 8 oz feta cheese, cubed
- ¼ cup sour cream
- ½ cup baby spinach
- ½ cup grated Swiss cheese
- 2 green onions, chopped
- 2 tbsp melted butter
- 4 tsp grated Parmesan cheese

1. Preheat air fryer to 320°F. Blend together feta, sour cream, spinach, Swiss cheese, and green onions in a bowl. Spread into the pan and Bake until hot, about 8 minutes. Unroll six of the breadsticks and cut in half crosswise to make 12 pieces. Carefully stretch each piece and tie into a loose knot. Tuck in the ends to prevent burning.
2. When the dip is ready, remove the pan from the air fryer and place each bread knot on top of the dip until the dip is covered. Brush melted butter on each knot and sprinkle with Parmesan. Bake until the knots are golden, 8-13 minutes. Serve warm.

Tasty Serrano Tots

Prep time: 5 minutes |Cook time: 30 minutes | Serves 4

- ¾ cup riced cauliflower
- 2 serrano peppers, minced
- 1 egg
- 1/3 cup grated sharp cheddar
- 1 oz cream cheese, softened
- 1 tbsp onion powder
- 1/3 cup flour
- ½ tsp salt
- ¼ tsp garlic powder

1. Preheat air fryer to 375°F. Mix the riced cauliflower, serrano peppers, egg, cheddar, cream cheese, onion, flour, salt, and garlic powder in a bowl. Form into 12 rectangular mounds. Add the tots to the foil-lined frying basket and Air Fry for 8-10 minutes.
2. Let chill for 5 minutes before serving. Enjoy!

Avocado Fries

Prep time: 15 minutes | Cook time: 10 minutes | Serves 8

- 60g plain flour
- Salt and ground black pepper, as required
- 2 eggs
- 1 teaspoon water
- 100g seasoned breadcrumbs
- 2 avocados, peeled, pitted and sliced into 8 pieces
- Non-stick cooking spray

1. In a shallow bowl, mix together the flour, salt, and black pepper.
2. In a second bowl, add the egg and water and beat well.
3. In a third bowl, place the breadcrumbs.
4. Coat the avocado slices with flour mixture, then dip into egg mixture and finally, coat evenly with the breadcrumbs.
5. Now, spray the avocado slices with cooking spray evenly.
6. Grease one basket of Ninja Foodi 2-Basket Air Fryer.
7. Press either "Zone 1" and "Zone 2" and then rotate the knob to select "Air Fry".
8. Set the temperature to 200 degrees C and then set the time for 5 minutes to preheat.
9. After preheating, arrange the avocado slices into the basket.
10. Slide basket into Air Fryer and set the time for 10 minutes.
11. After cooking time is completed, remove the fries from Air Fryer and serve warm.

Chili Corn On The Cob

Cook time: 30 minutes | Serves 4

- Salt and pepper to taste
- ½ tsp smoked paprika
- ¼ tsp chili powder
- 4 ears corn, halved
- 1 tbsp butter, melted
- ¼ cup lime juice
- 1 tsp lime zest
- 1 lime, quartered

1. Preheat air fryer to 400°F. Combine salt, pepper, lime juice, lime zest, paprika, and chili powder in a small bowl.
2. Toss corn and butter in a large bowl, then add the seasonings from the small bowl. Toss until coated.
3. Arrange the corn in a single layer in the frying basket. Air Fry for 10 minutes, then turn the corn.
4. Air Fry for another 8 minutes. Squeeze lime over the corn and serve.

Artichoke Samosas

Cook time: 25 minutes | Serves 6

- ½ cup minced artichoke hearts
- ¼ cup ricotta cheese
- 1 egg white
- 3 tbsp grated mozzarella
- ½ tsp dried thyme
- 6 phyllo dough sheets
- 2 tbsp melted butter
- 1 cup mango chutney

1. Preheat air fryer to 400°F. Mix together ricotta cheese, egg white, artichoke hearts, mozzarella cheese, and thyme in a small bowl until well blended. When you bring out the phyllo dough, cover it with a damp kitchen towel so that it doesn't dry out while you are working with it. Take one sheet of phyllo and place it on the work surface.
2. Cut it into thirds lengthwise. At the base of each strip, place about 1 ½ tsp of filling. Fold the bottom right-hand tip of the strip over to the left-hand side to make a triangle. Continue flipping and folding triangles along the strip. Brush the triangle with butter to seal the edges. Place triangles in the greased frying basket and Bake until golden and crisp, 4 minutes. Serve with mango chutney.

Thyme Sweet Potato Chips

Prep time: 5 minutes |Cook time: 20 minutes | Serves 2

- 1 tbsp olive oil
- 1 sweet potato, sliced
- ¼ tsp dried thyme
- Salt to taste

1. Preheat air fryer to 390°F. Spread the sweet potato slices in the greased basket and brush with olive oil. Air Fry for 6 minutes.
2. Remove the basket, shake, and sprinkle with thyme and salt. Cook for 6 more minutes or until lightly browned.
3. Serve warm and enjoy!

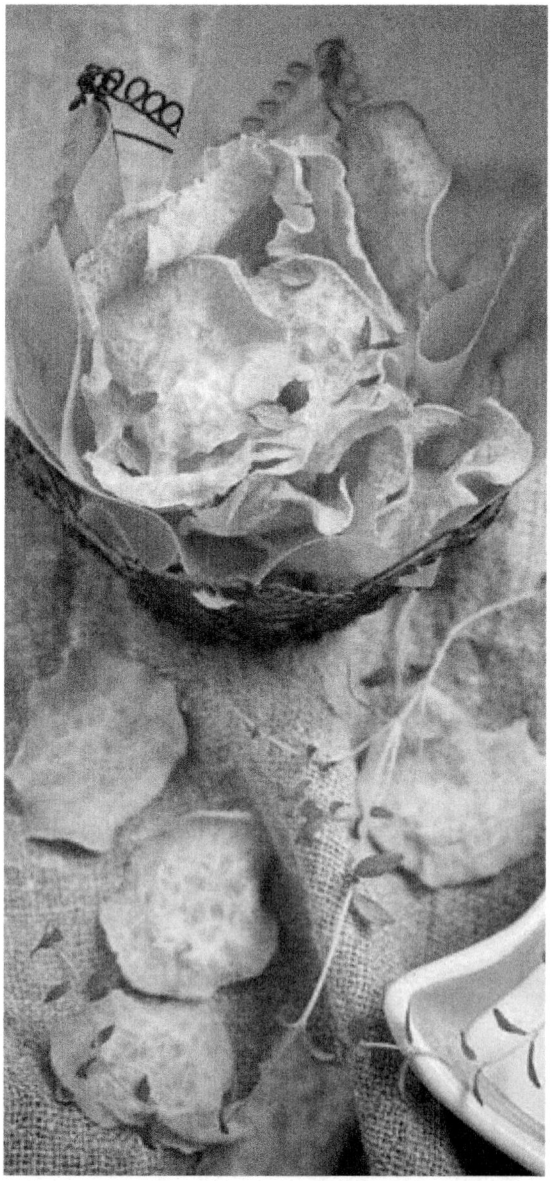

Pretzels Hot Dog

Prep time: 5 minutes | Cook time: 15 minutes | Serves 8

- 180ml warm water
- 2¼ teaspoons instant yeast
- 1 teaspoon sugar
- 2 teaspoons olive oil
- 250g plain flour
- ½ teaspoon salt
- 1 large egg
- 1 tablespoon water
- 8 hot dogs

1. Combine warm water, yeast, sugar, and olive oil in a large mixing basin to make the dough.
2. Stir everything together and leave aside for about 5 minutes.
3. Mix in roughly 125g flour and a pinch of salt. Add 125g of flour at a time until the dough comes together into a ball and pulls away from the bowl's sides.
4. On a floured board, pour the dough. Knead the dough for 3 to 5 minutes, adding extra flour until it is no longer sticky.
5. Cut the dough into eight pieces.
6. Roll the dough between your hands, and roll each piece into an 20 cm to 25 cm rope.
7. Pat, the hot dogs, dry with paper towels to make wrapping the dough around them easier.
8. Begin wrapping the dough around one end of each hot dog in a spiral. To seal the ends, pinch them together.
9. In a small mixing dish, whisk together an egg and a tablespoon of water. Coat the dough in egg wash from all sides.
10. Press your chosen zone - "Zone 1" or "Zone 2" and then rotate the knob to select "Air Fryer".
11. Set the temperature to 200 degrees C, and then set the time for 5 minutes to preheat.
12. After preheating, arrange pretzels into the basket of each zone.
13. Slide the baskets into Air Fryer and set the time for 8 minutes.
14. After cooking time is completed, place on a wire rack for a few minutes, then transfer onto serving plates and serve.

Asian Rice Logs

Prep time: 5 minutes |Cook time: 5 minutes | Serves 8

- 1½ cups cooked jasmine or sushi rice
- ¼ teaspoon salt
- 2 teaspoons five-spice powder
- 2 teaspoons diced shallots
- 1 tablespoon tamari sauce
- 1 egg, beaten
- 1 teaspoon sesame oil
- 2 teaspoons water
- ⅓ cup plain breadcrumbs
- ¾ cup panko breadcrumbs
- 2 tablespoons sesame seeds
- Orange Marmalade Dipping Sauce
- ½ cup all-natural orange marmalade
- 1 tablespoon soy sauce

1. Make the rice according to package instructions. While the rice is cooking, make the dipping sauce by combining the marmalade and soy sauce and set aside.
2. Stir together the cooked rice, salt, five-spice powder, shallots, and tamari sauce.
3. Divide rice into 8 equal pieces. With slightly damp hands, mold each piece into a log shape. Chill in freezer for 10 to 15minutes.
4. Mix the egg, sesame oil, and water together in a shallow bowl.
5. Place the plain breadcrumbs on a sheet of wax paper.
6. Mix the panko breadcrumbs with the sesame seeds and place on another sheet of wax paper.
7. Roll the rice logs in plain breadcrumbs, then dip in egg wash, and then dip in the panko and sesame seeds.
8. Cook the logs at 390°F for approximately 5minutes, until golden brown.
9. Cool slightly before serving with Orange Marmalade Dipping Sauce.

Jalapeño Poppers

Prep time: 5 minutes |Cook time: 5 minutes | Serves 18

- ½ pound jalapeño peppers
- ¼ cup cornstarch
- 1 egg
- 1 tablespoon lime juice
- ¼ cup plain breadcrumbs
- ¼ cup panko breadcrumbs
- ½ teaspoon salt
- oil for misting or cooking spray
- Filling
- 4 ounces cream cheese
- 1 teaspoon grated lime zest
- ¼ teaspoon chile powder
- ⅛ teaspoon garlic powder
- ¼ teaspoon salt

1. Combine all filling ingredients in small bowl and mix well. Refrigerate while preparing peppers.
2. Cut jalapeños into ½-inch lengthwise slices. Use a small, sharp knife to remove seeds and veins.
3. a. For mild appetizers, discard seeds and veins.
4. b. For hot appetizers, finely chop seeds and veins. Stir a small amount into filling, taste, and continue adding a little at a time until filling is as hot as you like.
5. Stuff each pepper slice with filling.
6. Place cornstarch in a shallow dish.
7. In another shallow dish, beat together egg and lime juice.
8. Place breadcrumbs and salt in a third shallow dish and stir together.
9. Dip each pepper slice in cornstarch, shake off excess, then dip in egg mixture.
10. Roll in breadcrumbs, pressing to make coating stick.
11. Place pepper slices on a plate in single layer and freeze them for 30minutes.
12. Preheat air fryer to 390°F.
13. Spray frozen peppers with oil or cooking spray. Place in air fryer basket in a single layer and cook for 5minutes.

Crispy Okra Fries

Cook time: 25 minutes | Serves 4

- ½ lb trimmed okra, cut lengthways
- ¼ tsp deggi mirch chili powder
- 3 tbsp buttermilk
- 2 tbsp chickpea flour
- 2 tbsp cornmeal
- Salt and pepper to taste

1. Preheat air fryer to 380°F.
2. Set out 2 bowls. In one, add buttermilk.
3. In the second, mix flour, cornmeal, chili powder, salt, and pepper.
4. Dip the okra in buttermilk, then dredge in flour and cornmeal.
5. Transfer to the frying basket and spray the okra with oil.
6. Air Fry for 10 minutes, shaking once halfway through cooking until crispy.
7. Let cool for a few minutes and serve warm.

Parmesan Crackers

Cook time: 6 minutes | Serves 6

- 2 cups finely grated Parmesan cheese
- ¼ teaspoon paprika
- ¼ teaspoon garlic powder
- ½ teaspoon dried thyme
- 1 tablespoon all-purpose flour

1. Preheat the air fryer to 380°F.
2. In a medium bowl, stir together the Parmesan, paprika, garlic powder, thyme, and flour.
3. Line the air fryer basket with parchment paper.
4. Using a tablespoon measuring tool, create 1-tablespoon mounds of seasoned cheese on the parchment paper, leaving 2 inches between the mounds to allow for spreading.
5. Cook the crackers for 6 minutes. Allow the cheese to harden and cool before handling. Repeat in batches with the remaining cheese.

Grilled Cheese Sandwich Deluxe

Prep time: 5 minutes |Cook time: 6 minutes | Serves 4

- 8 ounces Brie
- 8 slices oat nut bread
- 1 large ripe pear, cored and cut into ½-inch-thick slices
- 2 tablespoons butter, melted

1. Spread a quarter of the Brie on each of four slices of bread.
2. Top Brie with thick slices of pear, then the remaining 4 slices of bread.
3. Lightly brush both sides of each sandwich with melted butter.
4. Cooking 2 at a time, place sandwiches in air fryer basket and cook at 360°F for 6minutes or until cheese melts and outside looks golden brown.

Roasted Chickpeas

Prep time: 5 minutes |Cook time: 15 minutes | Serves 1

- 1 15-ounce can chickpeas, drained
- 2 teaspoons curry powder
- ¼ teaspoon salt
- 1 tablespoon olive oil

1. Drain chickpeas thoroughly and spread in a single layer on paper towels. Cover with another paper towel and press gently to remove extra moisture. Don't press too hard or you'll crush the chickpeas.
2. Mix curry powder and salt together.
3. Place chickpeas in a medium bowl and sprinkle with seasonings. Stir well to coat.
4. Add olive oil and stir again to distribute oil.
5. Cook at 390°F for 15minutes, stopping to shake basket about halfway through cooking time.
6. Cool completely and store in airtight container.

Appendix 1 Measurement Conversion Chart

WEIGHT EQUIVALENTS	
US STANDARD	METRIC (APPROXIMATE)
1 ounce	28 g
2 ounces	57 g
5 ounces	142 g
10 ounces	284 g
15 ounces	425 g
16 ounces (1 pound)	455 g
1.5pounds	680 g
2pounds	907 g

VOLUME EQUIVALENTS (DRY)	
US STANDARD	METRIC (APPROXIMATE)
⅛ teaspoon	0.5 mL
¼ teaspoon	1 mL
½ teaspoon	2 mL
¾ teaspoon	4 mL
1 teaspoon	5 mL
1 tablespoon	15 mL
¼ cup	59 mL
½ cup	118 mL
¾ cup	177 mL
1 cup	235 mL
2 cups	475 mL
3 cups	700 mL
4 cups	1 L

TEMPERATURES EQUIVALENTS	
FAHRENHEIT (F)	CELSIUS (C) (APPROXIMATE)
225 °F	107 °C
250 °F	120 °C
275 °F	135 °C
300 °F	150 °C
325 °F	160 °C
350 °F	180 °C
375 °F	190 °C
400 °F	205 °C
425 °F	220 °C
450 °F	235 °C
475 °F	245 °C
500 °F	260 °C

VOLUME EQUIVALENTS (LIQUID)		
US STANDARD	US STANDARD (OUNCES)	US STANDARD (OUNCES)
2 tablespoons	1 fl.oz	30 mL
¼ cup	2 fl.oz	60 mL
½ cup	4 fl.oz	120 mL
1 cup	8 fl.oz	240 mL
1½ cup	12 fl.oz	355 mL
2 cups or 1 pint	16 fl.oz	475 mL
4 cups or 1 quart	32 fl.oz	1 L

Appendix 2 Air Fryer Cooking Chart

Meat and Seafood	Temp	Time (min)
Bacon	400°F	5 to 10
Beef Eye Round Roast (4 lbs.)	390°F	45 to 55
Bone to in Pork Chops	400°F	4 to 5 per side
Brats	400°F	8 to 10
Burgers	350°F	8 to 10
Chicken Breast	375°F	22 to 23
Chicken Tender	400°F	14 to 16
Chicken Thigh	400°F	25
Chicken Wings (2 lbs.)	400°F	10 to 12
Cod	370°F	8 to 10
Fillet Mignon (8 oz.)	400°F	14 to 18
Fish Fillet (0.5 lb., 1-inch)	400°F	10
Flank Steak (1.5 lbs.)	400°F	10 to 14
Lobster Tails (4 oz.)	380°F	5 to 7
Meatballs	400°F	7 to 10
Meat Loaf	325°F	35 to 45
Pork Chops	375°F	12 to 15
Salmon	400°F	5 to 7
Salmon Fillet (6 oz.)	380°F	12
Sausage Patties	400°F	8 to 10
Shrimp	375°F	8
Steak	400°F	7 to 14
Tilapia	400°F	8 to 12
Turkey Breast (3 lbs.)	360°F	40 to 50
Whole Chicken (6.5 lbs.)	360°F	75

Desserts	Temp	Time (min)
Apple Pie	320°F	30
Brownies	350°F	17
Churros	360°F	13
Cookies	350°F	5
Cupcakes	330°F	11
Doughnuts	360°F	5
Roasted Bananas	375°F	8
Peaches	350°F	5

Frozen Foods	Temp	Time (min)
Breaded Shrimp	400°F	9
Chicken Burger	360°F	11
Chicken Nudgets	400°F	10
Corn Dogs	400°F	7
Curly Fries (1 to 2 lbs.)	400°F	11 to 14
Fish Sticks (10 oz.)	400°F	10
French Fries	380°F	15 to 20
Hash Brown	360°F	15 to 18
Meatballs	380°F	6 to 8
Mozzarella Sticks	400°F	8
Onion Rings (8 oz.)	400°F	8
Pizza	390°F	5 to 10
Pot Pie	360°F	25
Pot Sticks (10 oz.)	400°F	8
Sausage Rolls	400°F	15
Spring Rolls	400°F	15 to 20

Vegetables	Temp	Time (min)
Asparagus	375°F	4 to 6
Baked Potatoes	400°F	35 to 45
Broccoli	400°F	8 to 10
Brussels Sprouts	350°F	15 to 18
Butternut Squash (cubed)	375°F	20 to 25
Carrots	375°F	15 to 25
Cauliflower	400°F	10 to 12
Corn on the Cob	390°F	6
Eggplant	400°F	15
Green Beans	375°F	16 to 20
Kale	250°F	12
Mushrooms	400°F	5
Peppers	375°F	8 to 10
Sweet Potatoes (whole)	380°F	30 to 35
Tomatoes (halved, sliced)	350°F	10
Zucchini (½-inch sticks)	400°F	12

Appendix 3 Index

KATHLEEN C. MARTINS

Printed in Great Britain
by Amazon

17849385R00066